Praise for *Loyalty to Your Soul*

"Drs. Ron and Mary Hulnick are assisting the birth of something vastly important—an answer to the spiritual hunger that millions of individuals now feel. If you want to replace that gnawing emptiness in your life with a sense of meaning and fulfillment, **Loyalty to Your Soul** *is the guide you've been looking for. Written in crystal clear language, this book is a gem, and could only have been written by two people whose lives overflow with experience and wisdom."*

— **Larry Dossey**, M.D., the author of
The Power of Premonitions and *Healing Words*

"Ron and Mary Hulnick are the premier teachers and practitioners of Spiritual Psychology in the world today. The transformational Master's degree Program that they offer through the University of Santa Monica has changed thousands of lives. This book, so eagerly awaited, makes their work available to us all. It is truly a Rosetta stone for the Soul."

— **Joan Borysenko**, Ph.D., the author of
It's Not the End of the World and co-author of *Your Soul's Compass*

"With **Loyalty to Your Soul,** *Ron and Mary Hulnick give us a wonderful guide to what it really means to live a spiritual life, as well as a great thought system in Spiritual Psychology, which I believe will be the wave of the future and which they have been developing for the past 30 years. Having heard them speak at their home site, the University of Santa Monica—as well as having a partner who is a graduate of USM—I must say that Ron and Mary don't just teach these principles, they live them every day."*

— **Gary R. Renard**, the author of
The Disappearance of the Universe and *Your Immortal Reality*

*"**Loyalty to Your Soul** is the work of master teachers, two of the very best in our world. Ron and Mary Hulnick give us a step-by-step method and set of principles not only to overcome our egoic reactions, our upsets and fears, but to use as signals from our Souls as to what and how we can learn. Each problem serves as an awakener. We become Soul conscious as we apply the wisdom of the Soul to the problems of the ego. This is conscious self-evolution at its very best. A vital work for us all."*

— **Barbara Marx Hubbard**, author, evolutionary educator, and founder of the Foundation for Conscious Evolution

*"Bookstore shelves are filled with guides telling us how to get our bodies in shape, but there is very little practical advice about exercising our souls. Yet throughout America, millions seek to make their lives about something more than their own comforts and successes. **Loyalty to Your Soul** can be the handbook for that exploration. It tears down the false wall we've put up between our minds and our spirits, and shows the way toward a more fulfilling life."*

— **Arianna Huffington**, the cofounder and editor-in-chief of *The Huffington Post*

"I am grateful to Ron and Mary Hulnick for having written this book. They manage to make lofty spiritual principles clear and easy to understand, and they show you how you can apply them to your life. What more can you expect?"

— **Piero Ferrucci**, the author of *Beauty and the Soul*

"Reading Ron and Mary Hulnick's wonderful book of practical wisdom reminds the Soul of its inherent unity while lovingly guiding you, its manifestation in form, in discovering and fully living the call to Wholeness through your Soul's unique qualities."

— **Leonard Laskow, M.D.**, the author of *Healing with Love*

LOYALTY
TO YOUR
SOUL

Hay House Titles of Related Interest

YOU CAN HEAL YOUR LIFE, the movie, starring Louise L. Hay & Friends
(available as a 1-DVD program and an expanded 2-DVD set)
Watch the trailer at: **www.LouiseHayMovie.com**

THE SHIFT, the movie,
starring Dr. Wayne W. Dyer
(available as a 1-DVD program and an expanded 2-DVD set)
Watch the trailer at: **www.DyerMovie.com**

∽⠀∽

CHANTS OF A LIFETIME: Searching for a Heart of Gold,
by Krishna Das

INSPIRED DESTINY: Living a Fulfilling and Purposeful Life,
by Dr. John F. Demartini

*THE MOTHER OF INVENTION: The Legacy of Barbara Marx
Hubbard and the Future of YOU,* by Neale Donald Walsch

POWER vs. FORCE: The Hidden Determinants of Human Behavior,
by David R. Hawkins, M.D., Ph.D.

*SOUL LESSONS AND SOUL PURPOSE: A Channeled Guide to Why
You Are Here,* by Sonia Choquette

*SUPERCHARGED TAOIST: An Amazing True Story to Inspire
You on Your Own Adventure,* by The Barefoot Doctor

TIME FOR TRUTH: A New Beginning, by Nick Bunick

YOU CAN HEAL YOUR LIFE, by Louise L. Hay

YOUR SOUL'S COMPASS: What Is Spiritual Guidance?
By Joan Borysenko, Ph.D., and Gordon Dveirin, Ed.D.

All of the above are available at your local bookstore,
or may be ordered by visiting:

Hay House USA: **www.hayhouse.com**®
Hay House Australia: **www.hayhouse.com.au**
Hay House UK: **www.hayhouse.co.uk**
Hay House South Africa: **www.hayhouse.co.za**
Hay House India: **www.hayhouse.co.in**

LOYALTY
TO YOUR
SOUL

The Heart of Spiritual Psychology

H. Ronald Hulnick, Ph.D.,
Mary R. Hulnick, Ph.D.

HAY HOUSE, INC.
Carlsbad, California • New York City
London • Sydney • Johannesburg
Vancouver • Hong Kong • New Delhi

Published and distributed in the United States by: Hay House, Inc.: www.hay house.com • **Published and distributed in Australia by:** Hay House Australia Pty. Ltd.: www.hayhouse.com.au • **Published and distributed in the United Kingdom by:** Hay House UK, Ltd.: www.hayhouse.co.uk • **Published and distributed in the Republic of South Africa by:** Hay House SA (Pty), Ltd.: www.hayhouse.co.za • **Distributed in Canada by:** Raincoast: www.raincoast.com • **Published in India by:** Hay House Publishers India: www.hayhouse.co.in

Editorial supervision: Jill Kramer • *Project editor:* Patrick Gabrysiak
Design: Nick C. Welch

The entire poem titled "Someone Should Start Laughing" on pages 26 and 27 is reprinted verbatim as it appears on page 23 in the Penguin publication *I Heard God Laughing,* © copyright 1996 and 2006 Daniel Ladinsky and used with his permission.

The Rumi quote on page 200 is used with grateful permission of the translator, Coleman Barks.

The authors of this book do not dispense medical advice or prescribe the use of any technique as a form of treatment for physical, emotional, or medical problems without the advice of a physician, either directly or indirectly. The intent of the authors is only to offer information of a general nature to help you in your quest for emotional and spiritual well-being. In the event you use any of the information in this book for yourself, which is your constitutional right, the authors and the publisher assume no responsibility for your actions.

Library of Congress Cataloging-in-Publication Data

Hulnick, H. Ronald.
  Loyalty to your soul : the heart of spiritual psychology / H. Ronald Hulnick and Mary R. Hulnick.
    p. cm.
  ISBN 978-1-4019-2728-8 (tradepaper : alk. paper) 1. Psychology, Religious. 2. Spiritual life. I. Hulnick, Mary R., 1944- II. Title.
  BL53.H735 2011
  248.2--dc22

                                2010017079

Tradepaper ISBN: 978-1-4019-2728-8
Digital ISBN: 978-1-4019-2953-4

14 13 12 11   5 4 3 2
1st edition, February 2011
2nd edition, February 2011

Printed in the United States of America

To Dr. Neva Dell Hunter, who turned my life around and helped me find my Self; and to John-Roger, who turned my Self around and helped me find direction and inspiration for my life.

— **Ron**

To my mom and dad, Helen and Henry Holverson, for their constancy of Loving; and to John-Roger, whose exampleship has informed my life.

— **Mary**

INVOCATION

Since this book is about a spiritual orientation to life, we'd like to begin by inviting you to join us in setting a clear intention of receiving the greatest value possible from your experience with us. And the way we'd like to do so is by invoking the presence of Spirit to be with us as we share our time together.

Lord, God of all Creation, we ask now that we be cleared, filled, surrounded, and protected with the clear Light of the sacredness of Spirit. We ask for the presence, protection, guidance, and Love of the Divine Beings who work with each of us. And we ask that any imbalance that may be present in our consciousness be taken up into the highest realms of Light and Sound, where it may be transformed and used in Service. We are so grateful for this opportunity to come together in service to our growth, upliftment, and learning as we assist ourselves and each other on our way Home. Thy will be done. So be it.

CONTENTS

FOREWORD

One day when I was a very young man acting out in a very strange way, a friend said to me, "Neale, life doesn't come with a Little Instruction Book. You're on your own."

I always hated that thought. *Doggone it!* I shouted inside my head. *Life should come with a Little Instruction Book. And we shouldn't have to be "on our own." We should be able to get some help here. Surely somebody must know what's going on. . . .*

Well, somebody does. Ron and Mary Hulnick are very clear, and if *you* wish to be very clear, you will find it immensely satisfying to read this book.

Of course, there are many people who "know what's going on." We are blessed on this planet with many wonderful teachers. I found this out as the years went by. Yet few of these teachers have produced a book in which so much is made so understandable in so little time.

One read through these pages and I believe you will have all the information and tools you need to not only *understand* "what's going on" in this life, but also to begin to create what you *want* to have going on. Can there be a greater gift than that?

I think not, and so I am very grateful to both Mary and Ron; for through their wisdom, compassion, insight, experience, love, and soft genius, we are given answers here to just about every important question about life. Not only, *What's going on here?* but also, *Why am I experiencing what I'm experiencing?* and, more important, *How can I change my experience?*

I observe that most people waft in and out of clarity about these things throughout their lives. I know that I do. And sometimes it takes a little tug, an awakening, to pull us back from the edge of oblivion and out of the Cloud of Unknowing, returning us to ourselves—our True Self—in the process. I believe we are all, at some level, spiritual masters; and what can snap us back into this awareness can be the smallest thing: the chance utterance of a friend on the street, the lyrics to a song we hear on the radio, or a book that just happens to fall into our hands.

Now in my reality, books don't "just happen" to fall into one's hands. I believe that each of us is led to the right and perfect information at the right and perfect time. What we do with that information is another matter, but it's always being presented to us exactly when we need it.

That is what is happening here. Now all you have to do is convince your ego not to resist the miracle that you have found. It is the miracle of moving from your Mind to your Soul in the living of your life.

You should know that your ego will struggle mightily against any effort on your part to do this. Not because it is your enemy, but for quite the opposite reason: your ego is your friend, and it thinks it is protecting you from imagining that there is any other perspective better than the View of your Mind. Yet now comes this remarkable book, urging you to remain loyal to your Soul. Now come Mary and Ron Hulnick (do you think this is *by accident,* at just *this moment* in your life?) to promise you that life will change dramatically when you see the events of your day-to-day life through Soul-Centered Eyes, and then begin to *create* events from that space.

Ron and Mary are two people who have spent decades exploring how life works, joining other wonderful teachers in sharing what they've found through the extraordinary programs at the University of Santa Monica—a one-of-a-kind place where new messengers and healers are being educated, nurtured, and prepared through the crystal clear explanations and insights that are found here. (Ron is the President of that university, and Mary is the Chief Academic Officer.)

The Hulnicks don't say everything exactly as I would. There is some room, after all, in the Collective Creation for Individual Expression. And so, some of the things that they call *learning* I would refer to as *remembering,* and elsewhere they may say "to-MAY-to" while I say "to-MAH-to." So too might you find yourself differing just a tiny bit in the way that you behold certain experiences. But I'll bet you're going to say, "Of course! That's it! That's how it is!" to 98 percent of what you find in this book—and you are going to be deeply grateful that your search for True Self brought you here.

What we have in this work is the basis for an entirely new healing discipline: *Spiritual Psychology.* For centuries we have been using a psychological model based solely on the perspectives and perceptions of the mind. Here, at last, is a revolutionary departure from this thinking, which proposes that there are *other* perspectives and *other* perceptions that can be equally powerful in forming our reality and in mending humanity. This book presents one such perspective . . . perhaps, in fact, the most powerful of all.

For this striking contribution, we shall always be indebted to Ron and Mary Hulnick.

— **Neale Donald Walsch**
Ashland, Oregon

PREFACE

Why This Book—Why Now?
by Mary Hulnick

The moment Ron introduced himself to me, I became flustered, as I immediately knew he was going to be an extremely important person in my life . . . although I had no idea how. He was standing at the doorway to my classroom, waiting to ask if he could observe my class. He explained that he was an incoming doctoral student whose intention was to sit in on each of his upcoming professors' classes to get a sense of what he would be involved in throughout his three-year course of study. Quickly regaining my composure, I agreed.

Since the Department of Counseling and Educational Psychology at New Mexico State University was relatively small, it was certain that he would be in at least one of my classes each quarter, so I was not surprised to see him again at the start of the next term.

During the following three years, we gradually got to know each other. The bulk of our interaction was in the classroom, with an occasional office meeting to discuss a particular subject from a lecture. Of particular interest to me was the quality of Ron's consciousness. He raised thoughtful and evocative questions that required careful consideration before I answered. I eventually learned that he was a student of a spiritual teacher who had a small center some 65 miles away, to which he traveled each weekend to participate in the activities occurring there.

My weekends, on the other hand, were largely taken up by my rose garden. Although I was married, my husband and I had different interests, and mine involved visiting various nurseries and tending to my flowers. It was becoming clear that we'd probably go our separate ways before too long.

Three years came and went, and when Ron graduated in May of 1978, the department offered him a two-year position as a visiting assistant professor, which he accepted. They gave him the only available office in our department, which happened to be right next to mine. Naturally, Ron and I became friends.

By this time, my husband and I had decided to divorce. For some unknown reason, the completion of the divorce proceedings went on for several months longer than anticipated, even though everything was agreeable to both parties.

Then one day I received two phone calls within ten minutes of each other. The first was from my attorney, advising me that the paperwork was complete and all I had to do was come by his office and sign the documents. The second was from Ron, telling me that his spiritual teacher had just made her transition to the other side. The two calls seemed connected by fate; one chapter of my life was closing, as a new one was immediately opening.

In July of 1978, Ron and I attended a seminar in Los Angeles where we met spiritual teacher John-Roger. We recognized him as a person of extraordinary consciousness and found ourselves meeting with him shortly after the presentation. We spoke of many things, including the possibility that Ron and I might marry. He thought that this was an excellent idea since, as he put it, "your energies match and you could do a great deal of good work together."

We were married in January of 1979, which unexpectedly resulted in our leaving the university. I was being groomed to be the chair of the department, and it was simply not possible for a chair to have a spouse as a faculty member in the same department. Our intention was to work together, so the prospect of Ron accepting a research position or a staff position at the counseling center (both of which he had in fact been offered) was unappealing. Having no idea what we were going to do, I resigned.

The good news was that this resulted in a yearlong honeymoon, during which we enjoyed our two dogs and two cats, read a lot, delighted in magnificent southwestern sunsets, and developed many of the skills that would find their way into the programs we would eventually create.

At a certain point that year, we felt a need to meet with John-Roger, and it was then that he shared with us that several years earlier, he'd founded a university called Koh-E-Nor, which means "mountain of light." We didn't give this information much thought, as neither of us had any aspirations to start a school, nor any experience along those lines.

Several months later, I awoke quite early one day, having had a dream that Ron and I were to breathe life into the school John-Roger had mentioned to us. I shared my dream with Ron, and as soon as the clock struck 9 A.M., we called to request a meeting with John-Roger. That very next morning, we found ourselves driving to the El Paso airport, on our way to California to meet with him. We saw a beautiful double rainbow in the eastern sky that lasted for a long time, and took this as a portent of good things to come.

At the meeting, I shared my dream with John-Roger, and Ron and I both expressed our willingness to participate in Koh-E-Nor. He advised us that even though no classes had been taught, the school had been incorporated as a not-for-profit institution with the state of California. Similar to that famous line in *The Godfather*, he made us an offer we couldn't refuse: "If you've ever had a dream of starting your own school, and doing it the way you always wished it could be, here is the opportunity."

It didn't take very long to put our home in New Mexico on the market and move to California to embark on an amazing educational adventure. The first class graduated in 1982, 11 strong. Some 15 years ago, the name was changed to the University of Santa Monica (USM) and, as they say, the rest is history. Today, between 450 and 550 students participate in monthly classes in Spiritual Psychology.

౼౼

During these 30 years, thoughts of authoring a book came up from time to time. We had decided not to write one since we couldn't conceive of how to effectively put into words what is essentially an experiential process. Then one night Ron had a vivid dream in which John-Roger handed him a book with the word *Loyalties* written on the cover. The implication was clear. When we spoke with John-Roger, he simply said, "That wasn't a dream."

It's been about 12 years since that "dream," and *Loyalty to Your Soul* is the result. It contains many of the principles and some of the practices currently found in the two-year Master's degree Program in Spiritual Psychology at the University of Santa Monica, where I serve as Chief Academic Officer and Ron is President.

This book is co-authored by the two of us. However, since many of the stories are derived from Ron's experience, when the personal pronoun "I" is used, it's Ron's voice. When "we" is used, it is both of us speaking.

Regardless, all of the principles and skills presented are a compilation of co-created materials that we've spent the last 30 years developing.

And speaking of the word *we,* when this word is generally used, it may refer to humankind at large. We've done our best to distinguish between this meaning and when we're talking about ourselves, and hope you'll be able to discern which sense is intended in any given instance.

There's one more piece of information you may find useful: the stories sprinkled throughout the text are there to illustrate a particular point, and there are several that function more like *koans* (paradoxes to be meditated upon that spark intuition and enlightenment). These tend to be longer; and their aim is to draw you, the reader, in so that the story itself works to bring about a change of heart to assist you in shifting your consciousness.

Authors' Note: Throughout this book, there are many capitalized words that wouldn't normally be treated in this way. We've chosen to capitalize direct references to the Authentic Self as a way of distinguishing them from words used to reference the ego level. Our intention is for you, the reader, to recognize the capitalized words as Authentic Self qualities.

An additional anomaly you may wonder about is why we've capitalized and italicized the phrase *Seeing Through Soul-Centered Eyes*. We've done this to emphasize the importance of describing what occurs as an individual moves from normal "seeing" through physical eyes to *Seeing* from the vantage point of Higher Consciousness. Thus, these five words serve as a guiding principle toward which all of humanity is evolving.

INTRODUCTION

It's Time to Put Psyche Back into Psychology— as Well as the Rest of Life

Most people are struggling to make their way in the world.
Less obvious are those who are gracefully, joyfully,
and quietly easing their way out of it.

What an amazing and fantastic time to be alive, especially if you feel a deep yearning for something more relevant and meaningful than material success alone. There's little doubt that humanity is involved in a time of convergence, of something old dying while something new is being born. It could be called a global sea change, a worldwide paradigm shift.

As we see it, what is dying is the notion that advanced consumerism is the path to fulfillment. Many people are realizing that material abundance alone doesn't result in the happiness that endless marketing so consistently and enthusiastically promises. Dr. Bob Moorehead, former pastor of Overlake Christian Church in the Seattle area, cut to the quick of the "what's dying" matter when he penned:

> The paradox of our time in history is that we have taller buildings but shorter tempers; wider freeways, but narrower viewpoints. We spend more, but have less; we buy more, but enjoy less. We have bigger houses and smaller families; more conveniences, but less time. We have more degrees but less sense; more knowledge, but less judgment; more experts, yet more problems; more medicine, but less wellness. . . .

We have multiplied our possessions, but reduced our values. We talk too much, love too seldom, and hate too often. . . .

We've learned how to make a living, but not a life. We've added years to life, not life to years. We've been all the way to the moon and back, but have trouble crossing the street to meet a new neighbor. We conquered outer space but not inner space. We've done larger things, but not better things. . . .

We've conquered the atom, but not our prejudice. We write more, but learn less. We plan more, but accomplish less. We've learned to rush, but not to wait. We build more computers to hold more information, to produce more copies than ever, but we communicate less and less. . . .

These are the days of two incomes but more divorce; fancier houses but broken homes. . . . It is a time when there is much in the showroom window and nothing in the stockroom.

[Editor's Note: This quote has also been attributed to other people.]

"But what is being born?" you might ask. Might it be that humanity is witnessing nothing less than the emergence of a consciousness that the world has never seen? It's one that doesn't simply assume that happiness automatically results from obtaining material success. Rather, it's a consciousness that, first and foremost, asks essential questions such as:

- "Who am I?"
- "Why am I here?"
- "What is my life's purpose?"
- "How can I live a fulfilling life?"
- "How can I make a meaningful contribution in my world?"

Perhaps the single biggest event supporting this emerging perspective was the recent gathering of people participating via the Internet in a series of ten classes offered weekly by Oprah Winfrey and Eckhart Tolle. The classes paralleled the ten chapters in Tolle's best-selling book *A New Earth*. While estimates vary somewhat, it seems safe to say that somewhere between 12 million and 15 million people from around the world logged on to these discussions.

Other reports indicate that the sale of books and participation in conferences pertaining to spirituality are rapidly increasing. Even the rather conservative American Psychological Association recently added a new division: Division 36, Psychology of Religion. Its journal is titled *Psychology of Religion and Spirituality.*

What such individuals have in common is an enhanced awareness that there's more to life than what's on the surface; they're sensing a deeper level of reality operating. Many have come to the place where they're compelled to seek greater awareness of that reality, which is commonly referred to as *the spiritual.* They want to feel that their lives count for something, and to have the opportunity to make a meaningful contribution.

But where is the guidebook that shows how to live consciously within the context of spiritual reality? Where does one go to learn how to live successfully in a predominantly material-based reality while *Seeing Through Soul-Centered Eyes?*

The Soul of Psychology

Since psychology is our chosen field, we recently looked up the word *psyche* in the dictionary. What we found was: "breath, principle of life, soul." A great definition! Then we looked up the word *psychology.* We surmised it would follow that psychology would be the study of the psyche, but here's what we found: "the science of mind and behavior."

Wait a minute! What happened to the breath of life and the Soul? It wasn't there at all. Somehow what was intended as a study pertaining to the Soul got relegated to the province of the mind and behavior.

The spiritually focused approach to psychology that we study and practice at the University of Santa Monica is our way of asserting that it's time to bring *psyche* back into *psychology.* It's time to inhale the breath of life and bring the Soul back to its rightful place at the heart of psychology.

This is why the two-year Master's degree Program we offer is in Spiritual Psychology, which we define as "the study and practice of the art and science of human evolution in consciousness." It's a way of life that makes spiritual awakening the cornerstone of one's purpose. And while we're at it, might human beings also bring *psyche* back into all areas of our lives? Given that this appears to be the direction the world is going, what a wonderful time for the emergence of a truly Spiritual Psychology!

Loyalty to Your Soul presents a Soul-Centered context for living in harmony, with the conscious realization that all people are essentially spiritual beings. Many have come to the place in time where they're awakening into a spiritual reality that was previously reserved for a few advanced Souls. Within these pages, it's our intention to provide principles and practical tools to assist you in gaining the experience and awareness of how to live "into" a Soul-Centered reality, much as one would finally drive out of the fog and into the sunlight that was shining brightly all the while.

Our promise to you is that this book will provide you with keys you can use to live a life dedicated to your own spiritual progression—and do so within the structure of your current situation. Our hope is that your intention will be to contemplate the information and use the tools we present, for only by using them will you discover their true value. In these pages, you will have the opportunity to:

- Discover and explore what life looks like from the context of the Soul's reality, and understand how to use that awareness to live a more fulfilling life.

- Replace a chronic victim-centered "I am upset because . . ." view with an empowered *Learning Orientation to Life.*

- Release yourself once and for all from the emotional suffering that inevitably results from a small-self, ego-centered, judgment-prone perspective.

- Learn how a Soul-Centered approach automatically results in Love, Joy, Compassion, Acceptance, and Peace.

In the first few chapters, you'll be introduced to the context of what we refer to as spiritual reality and spiritual evolution, as well as some of the challenges individuals face as they awaken spiritually. You'll discover what a Learning Orientation to Life means and how the dynamics of consciousness operate.

Would you be surprised to discover that you have spiritual allies? You'll meet them midway through the book and find out how they operate and how to utilize them for your advancement. By this time, you'll be ready to hear all about taking the necessary steps to release yourself from emotional suffering, and then how to experience a life permeated with an enhanced awareness of your inherent worth and value. Also, sprinkled throughout are several easy-to-comprehend practices to help you reap the benefits of spiritual evolution for yourself.

In addition—and perhaps most important—you'll embark upon the adventure of exploring 22 principles of *Seeing Through Soul-Centered Eyes,* which will have the effect of transforming the way you see, approach, and experience life. These principles are spread throughout the book, and you may eventually find yourself joining the ranks of those who have been positively affected by embracing them. You'll understand how lives devoid of meaning became rich with meaning, while lives in a state of emptiness and separation became filled with a divinely orchestrated purpose.

As you progress through the book, you'll see how the vast majority of emotional suffering results directly from judgments born of illusion, misinterpretation, and misidentification, and how these can be surrendered in order to awaken to your inherent divinity. You'll discover how the problems and challenges you face can be viewed as *spiritual opportunities* when seen through Soul-Centered Eyes. As this occurs, you'll find that your life becomes richer—a much more meaningful and joyous adventure.

The good news is that everything you need is available to you in this very moment. You don't need anything or anyone else. Your future is truly in your own hands.

Effective Ways of Using This Book

There are basically three ways you can make good use of *Loyalty to Your Soul:*

1. The **first** is as a vehicle of *instruction.* You can use it to add to the sum total of information you are gathering related to spiritual awakening. This is a sound approach, as it allows your consciousness to consider concepts it resonates with, and which it may not have previously contemplated.

2. The **second** is as a vehicle of *education.* In this regard, you can implement the information in your daily life, thus converting it from knowledge to wisdom by experientially discovering for yourself what has validity for you and what doesn't. If you choose this approach, you'll want to engage in the simple processes presented within the chapters and experience your own realizations.

3. The **third** is as a vehicle of *connection.* The time you spend within these pages can provide an inner sanctuary where you can connect more deeply to, and partake of, the profound awareness and restorative power inherent in that which you truly are. In other words, when you are working with this book, you are much more likely to have the experience of *Seeing Through Soul-Centered Eyes.*

One of the methods we have found quite effective for deepening and strengthening this connection is writing spontaneous responses to certain evocative statements. At the end of each chapter, you will find one or more relevant "stem sentences" that we invite you to complete.

Here is an example of a stem sentence and some possible responses:

"As I learn to see myself and others through Soul-Centered Eyes . . ."

- ". . . I'll be more accepting of myself and others."
- ". . . I'll be less reactive to what other people say to me."
- ". . . I'll be more peaceful."

- "... I'll experience unconditional Love."
- "... I'll get to know God more intimately."

After reading each chapter, you can complete the stem sentences by writing whatever comes into your awareness. Respond to them over and over until you feel you have emptied all your thoughts on the subject at that time.

You may respond to a statement 5, 50, or 500 times. You're done when you *feel* done. This can take only one sitting, or may require several. You might work with the statement today and then again six months from now. Yours is a uniquely individual process, an experience to be honored and respected.

We strongly recommend that you write in longhand rather than on a computer. There's something about the act of writing that tends to access material from deep within. Your hand is physically connected with your nervous system, whereas your computer is not. Handwriting can be a fabulous tool for mining the inner treasures of your Soul Essence that we refer to as the "Authentic Self." Also, if you're like us, this is a great opportunity to use those special pens you've been collecting for years.

Some people light a candle and play quiet music as they write, as we're doing right now while drafting this Introduction. *How* you choose to do so is much less important than doing it. We do suggest that you get a special journal for this purpose, in recognition of the fact that you are involved in a sacred process. In this way, you'll be able to refer back to it from time to time and note changes in your thoughts, feelings, values, and priorities.

Regardless of how you use this book, please know that you are loved; for when all is written, said, and done . . . in the end there is only God!

(By the way, a by-product of engaging in this process of inquiry is that the quality of both your inner and outer life is likely to significantly improve!)

CHAPTER ONE

Light-Bearers Everywhere

*It's been said that when the student is ready, the teacher
will appear—and that's true. It's also true that when
the student is ready, teachers appear everywhere.*

I remember well the magical morning when I had my first conscious experience of awakening. It completely altered the course of my life, and opened up a level of awareness that I'd read about but never directly experienced. I was 33 years old at the time, and it occurred in a rather unusual way.

Questions about God

Prior to that day, and for as long as I could recall, I'd had a dilemma about God. For a while (mostly during my college years, but for some time after as well), I considered myself an agnostic. I just didn't know about God, and wasn't sure how to find out. I'd abandoned atheism, since it seemed to require the same level of faith in my *dis*belief as was necessary to hold a strong *belief* in God. It was just the other side of the same coin, and I had no such confidence either way.

And I envied those who did. For example, when Carl Jung was asked if he believed in God, he answered, "No, I don't believe . . . *I know.*" That knowing was what I longed for. I hoped that there was a God, because then, I thought, the world would make more sense. If a Supreme Being exists, there must be spiritual principles and guidelines for living. I wanted to know, not just cognitively, but experientially, the nature of Spirit and spiritual reality.

The college courses I'd taken in comparative religion and philosophy didn't provide satisfying answers, because the doctrines of the various religions often seemed contradictory. I couldn't understand how there could be so many different points of view on such an important issue. The more I read and studied, the more questions were raised in my mind. Finally, in frustration, I simply placed all of the different religions and philosophies onto a shelf and labeled it "Someday . . . maybe."

And what if there wasn't a God? Well, to me that seemed even more preposterous. It would mean that as humans we exist in a random, meaningless universe, leading lives with no ultimate purpose or significance other than those we created to suit ourselves. I wasn't a particularly happy camper and continued to wrestle with questions of purpose and meaning as I sallied forth from my undergraduate work into the real world of work.

I entered adulthood in Brooklyn, New York, where I'd lived most of my life. My quandary about God was still haunting me, and I found myself gravitating toward the field of psychology. I pursued and received a Master's degree in Clinical Psychology, but didn't find any satisfying answers there either. It all seemed so very . . . well, clinical.

Parapsychology, on the other hand, was exciting. Who wouldn't be curious about extrasensory perception, auras and channels, synchronicity, and the possibility of beings from other planets? It all seemed so very . . . well, mystical. And at this stage of my life, parapsychology represented a doorway into the unknown. Not quite the expected direction for the left-brained, logical, analytical sort of guy I fancied myself to be.

After all, I'd received my undergraduate training in experimental psychology. I spent a lot of time running rats through their paces in the lab, meticulously comparing how fast they could find their way out of mazes and observing how they became "conditioned" to press a bar in order to receive small pellets of food; I considered myself a scientist. As one of my most respected psychology professors used to say, "If you can't define something, you don't know what you're talking about." And yet, something beyond the rational, systematic domain of science was calling me. Something within me was not fitting into the narrow and limiting identification into which I was attempting to cram myself.

For example, I was the only student in the history of my college to ask if I could keep my lab rat at the end of the year. To everyone else, the little creature now knew the maze and was scientifically useless; therefore, he was soon to be euthanized, like all the others. But something in him called to me, so I took him home and named him Desi (in honor of Desiderius Erasmus, the humanitarian priest for whom my alma mater, Erasmus Hall High School, was named). At the time, saving Desi didn't seem to me to indicate a sentiment that was at odds with my scientific mind in any way. But in retrospect, it may have been a hint of things to come.

My Awakening Out West

One day my girlfriend at the time, Barbara, told me she was planning a trip to Taos, New Mexico, to visit her music teacher, who had recently moved there with his wife and young son. She invited me to go along, and I immediately agreed. Taos sounded like just the kind of place I should explore . . . and perhaps I might synchronistically encounter someone who had inside knowledge about the exciting field of parapsychology.

Once there, I asked people everywhere if they knew anyone who was into this field of study, and it was surprising to me that the answer was always no. But this was the late 1960s, some years before the New Age movement actively appeared on the scene.

Then one night while I was participating in a community drumming session, I asked my parapsychology question to a fellow drummer. To my surprise, he told me that he *did* know somebody. There was a woman down in Alamogordo, some 300 miles south of Taos, who was a "spiritual teacher."

Her name was Dr. Neva Dell Hunter, and the drummer gave me her phone number, suggesting that I call her office to schedule a consultation. I had been reading about spiritual teachers, and the thought of meeting one sent my drumming to a whole new level of enthusiasm that evening!

I called Dr. Hunter's office early the next morning and made an appointment. Barbara and I arrived the following day at Quimby Center, which turned out to be a small and very plain tract house on a modest street in Alamogordo.

A friendly young man named Robert, who was a student of Dr. Hunter's, greeted us at the door and invited us inside. When Barbara and I stepped into the living room, Dr. Hunter took one look at us and immediately called out to her secretary in a tone reserved for one who had just seen a ghost: "Betty, cancel all my other appointments for the day."

It was as though she had just recognized something she had been waiting for, and I thought her reaction a bit odd. Little did I know how that day would change my life.

Dr. Hunter, while somewhat overweight and older than I expected, seemed ordinary enough. We sat with her and a few of her staff in the living room and talked about many topics. I sensed nothing unusual about her until I expressed my interest in parapsychology. Then she began describing things about me that were impossible for her to know. It was as if she were reading from a file where my life story was archived. She just had way too much information about things I'd never discussed with anyone.

At some point in the conversation, she suggested that it would be of assistance to both Barbara and me to each have an *aura balancing.*

"A what?" I asked.

"Don't try to understand it with your mind," she said. "Just experience it, and then you can decide for yourself whether or not it has any value for you."

That sounded fair enough. After all, my mission here was to further my understanding of parapsychology, so what did I have to lose?

Robert would conduct the "balancing." Along with two other members of Dr. Hunter's team, designated as *Light-bearers,* he ushered me into a small room in which a sheet-covered massage table was set up. Robert explained that the purpose of the Light-bearers, in this instance, was to act as a spiritual battery by sitting silently and "holding the Light." He assured me that life is filled with Light-bearers, and explained, "They are the ones who assist us along our path. They seem to show up randomly, but really there is nothing random about it."

Robert asked me to take off my shoes and belt and lie down on the table on my back. The Light-bearers quietly sat down on chairs placed against the wall, closed their eyes, and began to meditate. *Innocent enough*, I thought.

After an opening prayer, Robert selected one of several quartz crystals, each attached to a small chain, which were neatly laid out on top of a short bookcase. He held the crystal over my stomach, and it began to turn counterclockwise even though his hand remained steady.

This went on for some time, and as I began to relax, I realized that I was actually feeling its motion in my body as it rotated. It was as if the crystal were somehow attached to something within me that could "feel" its movement.

Soon Robert began asking me questions. He wanted to know if I'd ever had a dream in which I was in prison. I wondered, *Where did that come from?* It wasn't even something that Dr. Hunter had brought up. How could he know that ever since I'd been a small child, I would occasionally dream that I was in prison and couldn't get out? I always awoke feeling frightened after these nightmares. I told all of this to Robert, and as he continued to hold the crystal, he simply asked, "Well, would you like to come out?"

"I'd like that very much."

"The door isn't locked," he told me. "All you have to do is open it and walk out." In my imagination, I did as he suggested. I pushed on the door, and indeed it swung open. I walked out.

Robert asked me to describe where I found myself and what I was experiencing. I said I was walking out of a building and into a beautiful meadow. I told him how free I felt. "Great," he said and proceeded with the next question, the crystal never missing a beat with its circular movement.

On and on it went, one question after another, for nearly three hours. Completing each series of inquiries resulted in an awareness of something opening and expanding in the area of my chest. This opening was accompanied by deeper and deeper feelings of peace; it was as if I had transcended my normal state of mind. In fact, for the first time in my life that I could recall, my mind was completely still.

When we were finished, Robert went out and got Dr. Hunter, who was in the living room talking with Barbara. Dr. Hunter entered the room, where I was still lying down, and inspected me from head to toe in a way I'd never seen anyone look at someone before. She was looking at *me,* yet at the same time she was looking at something else.

"Very good," she said to Robert.

Then she asked me, "Tell me, do you ever have the feeling that in relationships you give more than you receive?"

What a question! That was the story of my life.

"Always," I said. "That's always how I feel in relationships. I'm forever giving more than I'm receiving."

She paused for a moment and slowly said, "Well, my dear, I'm afraid what you're going to have to do is give more."

"What?" I nearly leapt off the table. "If I'm already giving more than I'm receiving, why would I want to give even more?"

She looked at me compassionately. "You see, the spiritual law is that we receive according to what we give. So if you feel that you're giving more than you're receiving, you're either giving less than you think you are, or receiving more than you think you are. Either way, to receive more, you must give more."

With those words, she left the room, and as strange as it seemed at the time, a deep calm came over me. I'd never experienced anything like this before. It was as if my heart had simply burst open, and out gushed a Love so enormous that it radiated outward in all directions and poured over everything. It encompassed the entire earth and beyond.

I'd simply fallen in Love with everything and everyone. I'd stepped into the consciousness that I'd read about but never known. Like Carl Jung, I was actually having the experience in which there was no more question about believing. I *knew!* In the astonishment of this realization, the only thing I could do was cry with tears of intense joy. I had come Home within myself. I *knew* without a doubt that God is Love, that Love is the basis of everything, and that Loving is the path of spiritual awakening.

Seeing Through Soul-Centered Eyes for the First Time

Slowly, with assistance, I got up off the balancing table and went outside. I wasn't exactly steady on my feet, so one of the Light-bearers accompanied me. After a short, silent walk, we went back inside.

When we returned, Barbara was having her aura balancing. While Robert worked with her, it was my turn to talk to Dr. Hunter. I had many questions, and she had infinite patience.

"Dr. Hunter, at the end of the balancing, you spoke of 'spiritual laws.' Are these laws universal? And if they are, what about all the different religions?"

She replied, "Unfortunately, many people confuse religion with spirituality. All the world's major religions, when used in the ways they were originally intended, are exquisitely beautiful paths that lay out specific practices and approaches to assist people in their quest for a greater awareness of their connection with God—in other words, to grow spiritually.

"Religions are forms. Think of an automobile. Let's say you want to go from here to Santa Fe: A car is a wonderful way to travel there, but it's when the car itself becomes the focus of attention that you're distracted and forget that this is just a means to reach your destination. People often take great pride in their cars, painting them different colors and adding all sorts of gadgets and frills. But all of that is irrelevant when your primary intention is to drive to Santa Fe.

"I'm afraid religions often become vehicles for separating one group of people from another, and both groups from God. You know, throughout history, more people have been killed in the name of God than for any other reason. Strange, isn't it?"

I nodded.

"Spirit, on the other hand, is the Essence behind religions." Dr. Hunter continued, "When people speak of spirituality, they simply mean awareness of the sacred reality of the Divine Essence within and beyond all creation.

"From a behavioral point of view, they often mean acting in ways that truly uplift oneself and others, regardless of race, color, creed, circumstance, environment, or religious persuasion—behaving as if we knew that God was observing our every move, which is a wise approach, since it happens to be true.

"Spiritual laws are indeed universal, Ron. They apply equally to all that exists—without exception. Think about gravity or sunshine; they both go on regardless of anyone's belief system. There's no requirement that you believe in them in order for you to walk on the earth or enjoy a sunbath. I like that."

I considered all she'd said, and then asked, "If there is a spiritual reality as well as spiritual laws, that would indicate that there must be a reason and a purpose for it all. What are we doing down here in these strange bodies, dealing with all the pain and emotional suffering that goes on?"

"That's a really good question," Dr. Hunter said, "and I'm afraid I can only give you a partial answer at this time. From a spiritual viewpoint, Earth is a school that Souls come to for the evolution of consciousness. All of us who are here earned the right to be enrolled as students, and there's a spiritual agenda or curriculum for each person. And it's really quite an accomplishment just to be here, a fact that's largely unknown to most of the world's population."

"So if we're in school, what are we supposed to be learning?"

She laughed. "I'm glad you said 'supposed to be learning,' since until we begin to become aware of the nature of—let's call it the *Earth School*—it's questionable whether very much *learning* is actually going on. To understand the Earth School, it's helpful to be aware that there are at least two levels of reality happening here simultaneously.

"The first is the one that we're most aware of, since it has to do with the physical world as we experience it through our five senses. This type of learning is generally goal directed, and it's what most people believe life to be about. So if you learn a new skill or a second language, the assumption is that you'll use what you've learned to somehow enhance the quality of your life and perhaps the lives of others. This type of education is largely instructional and geared for the mind and body. The results are to be utilized here on this planet."

I'd never thought about life in this way, but it made sense. "What's the second type of reality?" I asked.

"The second type has to do with spiritual progression itself—spiritual evolution, if you prefer—which is consciously knowing who you are and why you're here," she answered. "It has nothing to do with success in the physical world. Each Soul is aware of its own curriculum and will use all of life's experiences to further its spiritual evolution, which is simply another way of saying that one is becoming more and more aware of one's nature as a loving being. A Soul doesn't separate experiences into good or bad, right or wrong; it sees all of them as learning opportunities. And its main organ for sensing the world is the Spiritual Heart, which is characterized by Unconditional, Impersonal Love and Infinite Compassion.

"Since the Soul is Divine and has a Divine purpose, it's not particularly concerned with specific outcomes in physical-world reality. Furthermore, the Soul isn't limited to the five senses. It also uses a sixth sense, which we call *intuition;* and a seventh that we refer to as *direct knowing.* Most people know about intuition, but relatively few are aware of direct knowing. It's these last two senses that humankind is in the early stages of developing."

"Do you mean the Soul doesn't care whether or not we get what we want?"

"It only cares to the extent that the personality is aware of the Soul's purpose and has aligned itself in service to that purpose. Until that happens, the personality is mainly concerned with safety, comfort, and control, along with staying young and beautiful forever—or so it would seem based on what we see on TV."

"Dr. Hunter, you said that the Soul doesn't separate experiences into right and wrong or good and bad," I said. "But so much of life seems to be all about right and wrong. Is it the personality that does that?"

She nodded. "It's the personality or ego, if you will, that divides everything into right or wrong. The ego always wants to be right and will go to great lengths to prove its case. Its main organ for sensing the world is the mind. Since the ego operates within physical reality with worldly objectives, it's not at all concerned with whether the Soul learns its lessons or not. In fact, the ego only pays lip service to the Soul as it continues about its business of attempting to fulfill its many desires. Truth be known, the ego doesn't really believe that the Soul exists other than as a concept, since it sees itself as the center of the universe."

I contemplated her words, then shifted subjects. "What about aura balancing? Could I learn to do it, and how does it work?" I wanted to understand what I had just experienced and to be able to share it with others.

Dr. Hunter chuckled, and explained that balancing was an ancient healing technique that she had been taught by her inner teachers. Amazingly, in my current state of consciousness, this explanation made perfectly good sense.

As if she were reading my mind, she said, "You know, you don't have to be so concerned about understanding whether something is or is not so. All you really need to know is whether it works and, if it does, how to work *it*. In fact, 'what *is*' and 'what *works*' are really much better definitions of Truth than so-called factual accuracy.

"For example, take your experience with aura balancing. Prior to it, you had confusion in your mind about the reality of God. But now that you've experienced it, you have no doubt. Did something outside yourself change, or did a shift occur within you?"

"The latter," I admitted. "Outwardly, I'm no different than I was before. I'm just seeing everything through new eyes. It's as if I've been wearing glasses with distorted lenses, and now the filters have been removed. I've awakened into a level of awareness I've never been in before—one I never even knew existed."

Dr. Hunter agreed. "This is what happens when one begins to awaken. You literally see the world differently. Right now, you're *Seeing Through Soul-Centered Eyes*—eyes that are open to perceiving the second type of reality I spoke of that is hidden to most people.

Actually, you've had this awareness many times before. You just didn't recognize it for what it was because you had no conceptual reference by which to evaluate it.

"You've known about the reality of Spirit from the time you were born. That's why you've always questioned the meaning of life and why you majored in psychology. You thought this branch of study could provide the answers you were searching for—and at one time, it might have. Would it surprise you to know that the advent of psychology on Earth came about precisely because humanity lost sight of why we were here in the first place? It was intended to guide us back onto the true course of our life stream.

"Your inner Self has always been gently nudging you in the direction of spiritual awakening. All that's happened here today is that you've at last come to the place inside yourself where you're ready to awaken to the reality that you're a Soul having a human experience."

On and on it went, one revelation after another. Late in the afternoon, when Barbara's balancing was complete, we said our thank-yous and good-byes. I was profoundly grateful. As I left, Dr. Hunter's parting words were: "You're probably going to want to come back here at some point. Please know that you're always welcome."

✐✐

A Soul having a human experience! Little did I realize that those six simple words would launch me on a lifelong journey. After more than 40 years, I'm still inspired every time I think of them. They serve to ground me as I continue venturing forth into the ever-expanding vastness of consciousness.

And thus we have arrived at the first principle inherent in Spiritual Psychology—or, said another way, what we observe when we see through Soul-Centered Eyes:

> ***Principle #1:*** *We are not human beings with Souls;*
> *we are Souls having a human experience.*

As Robert mentioned before beginning my aura balancing, Light-bearers are those we encounter throughout our lives who somehow play a significant role in our awakening. In this chapter alone, I count a total of 11 specific Light-bearers mentioned, beginning with Carl Jung—and, of course, including my wonderful white rat, Desi, who took me beyond science and into Love.

As a postscript, I did indeed take Dr. Hunter up on her invitation to return to New Mexico. And since that amazing day, I have never again dreamed that I was in prison.

Stem Sentences to Write Down and Contemplate

- Light-bearers in my life include . . .
- If I'm a Soul having a human experience, then . . .

Repeat as often as necessary.

CHAPTER TWO

Waking Up Is Not So Easy; It's Also Not So Hard

Actually, there's no spiritual path or spiritual journey. There's only where one is in the process of spiritual awakening. Thus, the physical world is a temporary place. Like a job, it's filled with opportunities.

At the beginning of the 19th century, poet William Wordsworth, in his classic *Ode: Intimations of Immortality from Recollections of Early Childhood*, wrote:

> *Our birth is but a sleep and a forgetting:*
> *The Soul that rises with us, our life's Star,*
> *Hath had elsewhere its setting,*
> *And cometh from afar:*
> *Not in entire forgetfulness,*
> *And not in utter nakedness,*
> *But trailing clouds of glory do we come*
> *From God, who is our home . . .*

Don't you love the beautiful line "Not in entire forgetfulness"? In other words, Wordsworth is saying that human beings are not *totally* asleep; someplace deep inside of us remembers "God, who is our home." And it is this recollection—this inner sense—that we are seeking to strengthen and make ever more conscious. It is this process of remembering that is what we mean by awakening.

Let's be clear: In this book, we're not talking about a poetic promise of a heavenly paradise after death that awaits those of us who have earned and deserve it.

Rather, this is about waking from your "sleep and a forgetting" right here and now while you are still very much alive. Not only can you awaken from your sleep, it is your *destiny* to do so. But first you must remove the blinders from your eyes.

The Lessons of Unlearning Begin

When I left Alamogordo and reentered my everyday life, I slowly began to assimilate my Quimby Center experience. I found myself frequently contemplating the enormous implications of what it means to be a Soul having a human experience. I realized that, in a very real sense, I was not the same person I had been before my encounter with Dr. Hunter. Actually, I was the same person; I was just seeing things differently.

I'd gained access to an inner spiritual reality, and the experience was nothing like I thought it would be. In my imagination, I'd anticipated that great stores of knowledge would instantly open up to me, and I'd become an all-knowing font of wisdom. Instead, it was like walking out from a dark room into brilliant sunshine and being bathed in a Light whose Essence is Love. What I thought I was seeking was unlimited knowledge; what I found instead was limitless Love.

Given Dr. Hunter's parting words—"You're probably going to want to come back here at some point. Please know that you're always welcome"—it was not a complete surprise that within a few months of returning home, my life began to unravel.

I'd left New York the previous year and was living in my beloved Vermont, but my relationship with Barbara ended. I would awaken every morning in a state of extreme anxiety, and it would take several hours for it to pass. I was becoming depressed. The only place I could imagine finding help for myself was at Quimby Center, so I called Dr. Hunter and asked if I could come back. She said, "Certainly," and off I went.

When I arrived in Alamogordo, it didn't take very long for me to realize that nothing less than becoming one of her full-time staff members and students would suffice, so I rented my Vermont property and moved to New Mexico.

One of the things I learned very quickly was that Dr. Hunter had some interesting and rather unorthodox ways of working with her students to help with the process of unlearning in general and loosening the reins of the ego in particular. One afternoon stands out in my memory.

Because she had some morning appointments that took longer than anticipated that day, we—the Quimby staff—found ourselves having a rather late lunch. It was 3 P.M. by the time we were finished doing the dishes. (Dishwashing, incidentally, was training in the discipline of making no noise since Dr. Hunter was very sensitive to sound. It was also an exercise in water conservation, because, after all, we were living in the desert.) Just as the last plate was put away, she nonchalantly announced that it was time to begin preparing for dinner, as she had some guests coming and they would need to dine at 4:30. "But Dr. Hunter," we sputtered with an astonished and righteous tone, "we've just had lunch!"

"I'm well aware of that," she said. "But if you're going to learn how to work in the Light, you must learn not to be controlled by habit patterns. You must learn how to live in the present and act in accordance with what the present requires of you. And right now, it requires that we get ready for dinner."

While dinner a few hours after lunch was a hard lesson for my ego to swallow, much less my stomach, it's true that as one begins to shift in consciousness from ego identification to Soul identification, the ego loosens and ultimately relinquishes control. This letting go is sometimes done easily, but more often it's accompanied by much kicking and screaming.

How Much Sleep Is Enough?

An easier lesson for me was the business of breaking sleep habits. I grew up with the quaint notion that seven to eight hours of rest each night was necessary for me to function well during the day. Further, I had the absurd belief that those hours should come around the same time every night.

Dr. Hunter didn't seem to see it that way at all. It's not that she ever said she disagreed; she just lived as if those sleep rules didn't exist. And since we lived around *her* day, the rules ceased to exist for us as well.

One of her favorite tactics was to begin a class with us around 11 P.M., after we'd all put in a pretty long day around the Center. Ostensibly, it was billed as a time for just being quiet together to review events from the day, so about six of us would tend to gather in her living room and talk. When a pertinent point emerged, she would often ask someone to read out loud from a book we were studying.

Late one night, she asked me to read, which I happily did. I was really engrossed in what I was reading and looked up after only a few pages to see if anyone might have a question or a comment. Much to my amazement, everyone's heads, including Dr. Hunter's, were tilted to one side or the other. *They all seem like they're sound asleep,* I thought. *What should I do? Keep reading out loud to myself?* I decided to see if they were, in fact, out cold. So I continued reading: "Spirit may work with people in many ways, one of which is through a 50-foot pink hippopotamus . . ."

I awaited a response, but not a creature stirred! While I had a lot of fun that night, I once again got to bed around 2 A.M., with just enough time for a nap before I was scheduled to be back at the Center at 7 that same morning. After several months of this, it became clear to me that while my ego may have thought it needed seven or eight hours of sleep, the part I was awakening into needed far less.

Over time, I came to experience more fully what all people do at some point in their awakening process. It is the realization (to see with *real eyes*—eyes that see what is real) that another seat of consciousness exists within that functions apart from our egos and responds very differently to many of life's situations. As the process continued, I slowly began to learn how to utilize my ego in a more useful way to successfully negotiate the physical-world reality in service to my newly discovered, spiritually oriented Self.

And believe me, most of those lessons involved "unlearning."

My time with Dr. Hunter encompassed five years and ended when she made her transition. I was at her bedside when she took her last breath, and I am eternally grateful for all that she taught me.

A New Way of Seeing

It took me years to integrate this new way of seeing and being in the world. During that time, I began devouring volumes of reading material pertaining to spiritual awakening, attending many seminars, and listening to countless lectures.

I knew that I'd opened up to a place within my consciousness that many others had discovered before me. I'd unlocked the doors to a level of awareness and state of being that, years later, I would come to know as the Authentic Self. And from this place, I finally understood the words attributed to the 20th-century Irish Taoist philosopher Terence Gray, who published under the name Wei Wu Wei, which fascinated me from the moment I first read them:

> "Why are you unhappy?
> Because 99.9 per cent
> Of every thing you think,
> And everything you do,
> Is for yourself—
> And there isn't one."

He was conveying that, contrary to popular belief (just as much then as now), the self we *think* is in charge of "minding the store" is really an illusion. Oh, it's real enough as we spend time marketing, stocking the shelves, taking inventory, and assessing profit, but these things aren't the Soul's reality. They're not how the Soul *sees* the world. To the Soul, it matters little if the store is minded at all. The Soul is using it—as well as all aspects of earthly experience—for its purpose: to grow in wisdom and deepen in Loving. And thus, through my experience at Quimby Center, I realized a second important principle of *Seeing Through Soul-Centered Eyes:*

Principle #2: *The nature of God is Love!*

Of course, the great avatars and mystics have been giving us this message since the dawn of recorded time. I'd read their stories on many occasions, and each time their words touched someplace deep inside that resonated with their truth. But it wasn't until I had the conscious experience of awakening into a realization of my own spiritual nature that I truly experienced the meaning of what I'd been reading.

Over time I came to understand that this simple truth reveals an *evolutionary direction,* which is toward Essence. It was this single awareness that became the cornerstone for what we now call Spiritual Psychology. What followed this insight was a process for moving forward spiritually, which we'll discuss in upcoming chapters.

Waking Up

When thinking of waking up, it's natural to imagine going to sleep at night and rousing ourselves in the morning. While we're asleep and dreaming, our dream experience is real. But when we wake up, *that* state is now real and the dream recedes.

Waking up spiritually is much the same, for as Dr. Hunter pointed out, there are two apparently disparate realities occurring simultaneously: (1) physical five-sense reality, and (2) spiritual reality. For the purpose of this book, when we discuss waking up, we're talking about the experience of shifting awareness so that one becomes more cognizant of, and attuned to, the dimension of spiritual reality. And an essential step in this direction is developing the awareness of the context of how life looks when *Seeing Through Soul-Centered Eyes.*

It's not that there are actually two separate realities in parallel positions happening next door to each other. It's more like a play being acted upon a stage where all of the actors believe that what they're experiencing is real. The audience, however, is aware that what they're observing is a play. And it's not that the play isn't happening, because it is in physical-world reality. It's just that the concerns in the lives of the people watching it transcend the issues of the characters in the play. For the most part, the audience members, no matter how engrossed they are in what the actors are doing, never forget that they have lives outside the theater. They don't leave hoping the suffering stage characters will get their act together. (No pun intended.)

In much the same way, physical-world reality happens within the larger context of spiritual reality. In other words, spiritual reality encompasses everything in physical reality, plus more. And it is the *more* that's the focus of those involved in spiritual awakening. I love the way Zen teacher Charlotte Joko Beck says, "You cannot avoid paradise. You can only avoid seeing it."

Believing and Knowing

The challenge you have prior to awakening is that no matter how much you may want to believe in spiritual reality, it isn't until you've had the inner experience that the "doors of perception," as William Blake put it, open to realms you didn't know existed. Prior to awakening, you can only believe, disbelieve, question, or doubt—which are all mind-based functions. However, once you awaken, all these illusions simply fall away and are replaced by undeniable knowing.

To grasp the distinction between believing and knowing, imagine yourself blindfolded and escorted to a room where you're told that someone you love is silently waiting for you. Further, you're placed in a chair and told not to move or attempt to communicate with this person in any way.

Because your usual five-sense modalities are rendered useless by the conditions imposed, you're unable to verify his or her presence. Your choices are to believe, disbelieve, doubt, or simply remain unaware of whether or not your loved one is present.

Once you're allowed to remove the blindfold, you can easily determine for yourself whether or not someone is there. All of your beliefs will now be replaced with the certainty of knowing through direct experience. It is this direct experience of spiritual reality for which we all yearn. It also translates to the third principle of Spiritual Psychology:

Principle #3: *Direct experience is the process through which belief or faith is transformed into knowing.*

This is what Carl Jung meant when he said he didn't *believe* in God; he *knew*. Spiritual teacher John-Roger said it this way: "If you're going to go inside yourself, you have to go in and contact a separate reality other than the reality you're familiar with. That separate reality will be the Spirit."

Religion and Spirituality

Merriam-Webster's Collegiate Dictionary defines *religion* as "the service and worship of God or the supernatural." Broadly speaking, religion refers to a set of beliefs and practices designed to help the faithful enter heaven and reside with God for eternity. Generally, such reward is thought to be received after bodily death, and only by the faithful.

The same dictionary defines *spiritual* as "relating to, consisting of, or affecting the spirit." Spirituality, as we define it, has to do with the process of awakening into the conscious experience of unconditional Love in the here and now, rather than only after one dies. In this context, spiritual progression and evolution are one and the same.

It's important to recognize that all major religions accept unconditional love and compassion as their core teaching. For this reason, there's no need to argue over the fundamentals of any particular religious perspective. They're all valuable to the degree that people use them to evolve into a greater awareness and manifestation of their own inherently loving and compassionate nature.

What spirituality does *not* mean is using one set of beliefs and practices as a justification for behaving negatively toward others because they happen to believe differently.

A magnificent example of convoluted religious logic, which unfortunately is all too common today, is presented in Dan Brown's best-selling novel *The Da Vinci Code*. Readers are introduced to a character named Silas who considers himself a Christian soldier. Brown gives us a glimpse into Silas's mind:

> *Jesus' message is one of peace . . . of nonviolence . . . of love.* This was the message Silas had been taught from the beginning, and the message he held in his heart. And yet *this* was the message the enemies of Christ now threatened to destroy. *Those who threaten God with force will be met with force. Immovable and steadfast.*

Silas sees no contradiction. He fails to recognize that Christ did not meet force with force, but with Love. He does not understand that pitting one set of religious practices and beliefs against another goes against the very nature of what he believes in. One of the clearest articulations of this truth came from former President Bill Clinton:

> The real differences around the world today are not between Jews and Arabs; Protestants and Catholics; Muslims, Croats, and Serbs. The real differences are between those who embrace peace and those who would destroy it; between those who look to the future and those who cling to the past; between those who open their arms and those who are determined to clench their fists.

Compounding the confusion are reports in the media that deal with *religion* and *spirituality* as interchangeable terms. For instance, when levels of spirituality in the general population are measured, it's often the frequency of variables such as church attendance, Bible study, or prayer that are used as leading indicators. Yet these variables may indicate adherence to religious form rather than authentic spiritual practice. In other words, the measure of people's religious merit is generally determined by the faithfulness of their outer worship. And while some religious practices may result in enhanced levels of spiritual awareness, some, like what Silas did, may not.

On the other hand, people's spiritual growth can be gauged by results experienced *within* and how they choose to lead their lives. These developments may occur suddenly and spontaneously, often during spiritual practices such as prayer, meditation, or selfless acts of service.

However, rare is the research that uses an individual's level of unconditional Love and Compassion as a measure of spirituality. Why? For one thing, levels of Love and Compassion are much more difficult to measure.

As we've said, some religious practices may result in enhanced levels of spiritual awareness, and some may not. This can be thought of as the distinction between *form* and *essence*. In other words, regardless of what you claim to believe or what rituals you perform, progressing spiritually, in the context of Spiritual Psychology, means learning to live in ways that demonstrate enhanced levels of Love and Compassion for yourself and others.

Another example of this confusion can also be found in the political debate regarding the separation of church and state. There's general agreement that the intention of the drafters of the Constitution was to prohibit any single religion from becoming a dominating force in the governance of the U.S. So far, so good, as this was the intent of our Founding Fathers.

The confusion sets in when the meaning of the Constitution is also taken to mandate a separation of spirit and state. The First Amendment says: "Congress shall make no law respecting an establishment of religion, or prohibiting the free exercise thereof . . ." The debate in this area appears to focus on the first part of the amendment, but the second part clearly stipulates support for all religions. Separating a single religious persuasion from secular government makes sense. But a government that isn't operating in harmony with principles based on encouraging, supporting, and enhancing levels of Love and Compassion by and for all is another matter entirely.

The Challenges of Awakening

Just as people spend a large portion of their lives sleeping and dreaming, they also live with one foot in the everyday physical world and the other in a spiritual slumber. The astonishing thing is that as you wake up to the dimension of spirit, you become aware that others are awakening, too. There are many people—their eyes still bleary from sleep—looking around and wondering what to do now that they've discovered that there are aspects to human existence vastly more valuable than material success. How do you live in a world where all of a sudden everything looks familiar . . . yet, at the same time, quite different? Will you function differently when you *see* through Soul-Centered Eyes? As poet David Whyte put it, "Revelation must be terrible with no time left to say goodbye."

There are a number of challenges you'll face when awakening. Being aware of some of them is helpful, as this provides a conceptual context that can help allay the sense of fear and concern that often accompanies the experience. Here are eight of the most common:

1. The Challenge of Cognitive Dissonance

When you begin to see the world in a different light, it can be extremely disconcerting to hear new ideas that ring true inside. Yet at the same time, these new ideas may contradict fundamental beliefs you have been conditioned to cling to. This simultaneous holding of contradictory ideas is what's meant by *cognitive dissonance*.

And make no mistake, this challenge alone can be so shocking that many people discount the awakening experience, lay their heads back down on their pillows, and go back to the familiar comfort—or discomfort—of their sleep. This is an understandable impulse since, in the Spirit-Centered context, everything takes on new meaning and is reevaluated and rewoven into a brand-new tapestry of life. Engaging and appreciating this process takes time, energy, and commitment. And the awareness you come to may challenge your whole way of life and prompt you to make some fairly radical changes. In fact, as you awaken, shifts in perception are often accompanied by amazing enlightenment as the miraculous becomes the ordinary.

Thoreau wrote: "The mass of men lead lives of quiet desperation." His observation mirrors our own. So many in these challenging times appear to be sleepwalking, misunderstanding what their veiled eyes perceive. But the fact is, ignorance is *not* bliss.

And once you become aware of your own spirituality, you can never again lose that recognition, for there is no ignoring the deeper truths once you've experienced them.

2. The Challenge of Surrendering the Illusion of Control

John-Roger has called control the "master addiction," and this appears to be a very accurate description. Everywhere you look, you can see publication after publication extorting you to take control over this and that and everything in between, promising that, as you do so, the quality of your life will be much more to your liking.

What's at stake in surrendering this illusion involves nothing less than the fear of abandonment and of losing touch with reality. Control is based on the ego's search for comfort, safety, and security; and its effort to hold everything in place. It's basically a survival mechanism marketed as a means to attain what most people desire—especially money, sex, and power. The ego creates a picture of the ideal way things (life, the world) should be, and then it uses control to try to make reality match its ideal.

3. The Challenge of Freedom from Identification with Roles and Personal History

What do you do when you recognize that the roles by which you used to define yourself no longer suffice, and you begin existing beyond them? How will you be in the world when you realize that you're no longer so strictly identified by wearing hats such as "father," "mother," "banker," "golfer," "activist," or anything described in terms of physical-world reality?

How will you function when you see that, first and foremost, you're a spiritual being who has put on the role of, say, business executive in exactly the same way you would put on a particular suit for the day? Ironically, it's also notable that as you awaken, you find yourself functioning more consciously within your chosen roles.

As you grow into the realization of yourself as a spiritual being residing in eternity, you find your entire sense of personal history receding into the background. As you become more aware of who you are, your attachment to your past, and identification with it, becomes less and less.

I was talking with Dr. Hunter one day and asked her about my background. I shared that although I was raised in the Jewish tradition, I didn't experience much of a connection with the religion.

"Well," she replied, with that small smile I had come to treasure, "you know how it says in the Bible: 'Come ye out from among them'?"

I nodded, and she went on, "You had to come out from somewhere. Actually, whatever our lineage, as we experience our awakening we become an example for those coming after us of what it means to step free of form into essence."

4. The Challenge of Continuing to Participate

It used to be that when people had this sort of transformational experience, they renounced material life, moved to the local ashram, took vows of non-possession, and spent the remainder of their days living a monastic and contemplative life in service to knowing God.

However, in today's world, when unprecedented numbers of people are waking up simultaneously, there just aren't enough beds at the ashram to go around. It's as if the Berlin wall of spirituality has come crashing down and millions are poised to rush through. But there are mouths to feed, kids to send to college, elders requiring care—numerous responsibilities we wish to honor. We must continue to fulfill these obligations; it's just that we learn to do so from a different place inside.

At the same time, life no longer makes sense the way it used to. For one thing, the material motivation that used to power your life may suddenly run out of energy. In *A Separate Reality*, by

Carlos Castaneda, don Juan referenced this phenomenon when he described the daily activity of the "man of knowledge" as "controlled folly." This challenge involves nothing less than learning how to be in the world but not of it.

5. The Challenge of the Inadequacy of Words

Complicating the situation further, you discover that your vocabulary is inadequate to the task of sharing your experience with those in your life who have not had a similar experience. Words you used to use now have different meanings, as the meanings of words change at different levels of awareness.

For example, in physical-world reality, the word *love* usually means a certain degree of intimacy and closeness with another. It's indicative of a very personal shared experience.

In spiritual reality, the word *Love* embraces personal love, but also transcends it. It's far more expansive, all-inclusive, and unconditional. In the context of spiritual reality, Love is like gravity—it encompasses and attracts everything! It's the very nature of the Essence of our core. And it's what "You shall love your neighbor as yourself" in Matthew 22:39 is all about.

Perhaps this is why the deeper Soul-Centered meanings of life have often been communicated through music, poetry, art, and storytelling, since they bypass the analytical mind and small, self-centered reality. A great example of this is how Jesus often spoke in parables. Spiritual reality is not something that can be explained directly with words. As the Persian mystic and poet Hafiz put it:

I have a thousand brilliant lies
For the question:
How are you?

I have a thousand brilliant lies
For the question:
What is God?

If you think that the Truth can be known
From words,

If you think that the Sun and the Ocean

Can pass through that tiny opening
Called the mouth,

O someone should start laughing!

Someone should start wildly Laughing—Now!

(From the Penguin publication: *I Heard God Laughing,* copyright 1996 & 2006 Daniel Ladinsky and used with his permission.)

6. The Challenge of Speed and Noise

Have you ever wondered why it tends to be quiet in places of worship? Or why you've been advised to listen carefully to the still, small voice that speaks within? Or why individuals attend silent spiritual retreats? Might there be a relationship between awakening, solitude, and silence?

As it turns out, it is in the stillness that Love is found. Unfortunately, life is filled with noise, rapidity, and distraction. Speed is everywhere. Nowhere is this trend more evident than in measurements of the attention span of people in general, and children in particular. There's even a name for it: *attention deficit disorder.* Further, there doesn't appear to be any end in sight. Multitasking is the order of the day. And now, with the advent of cellular phones that send and receive text messages, there's no easy escape without perhaps appearing irresponsible. And to make matters even worse, there's no longer any doubt that what's referred to as an "elevated level of stress" is a major contributor to many, if not all, diseases.

For the awakening person, there is a growing yearning for time in the silence. There is a sense of needing time and space for contemplation, meditation, walking in nature, and just plain being alone. Attuning to the inner channel of Divine Love is supported by quiet moments.

That this is easier said than done is evidenced by the phenomenon of going on vacation and not knowing what to do. We also hear from those who successfully slowed down on a holiday only to be confronted with the daunting task of needing to speed up upon reentry back into their "normal" lives.

7. The Challenge of Holy Man's Disease

Once you have begun the spiritual quest and learned a bit of spiritual jargon, there's the trap of thinking that this so-called knowledge has instantly transformed you into an enlightened guru. It can be difficult to see that, in actuality, the ego in its self-proclaimed superiority is arrogantly parading its desire to maintain its sense of self-importance. There's a tendency to proclaim what you've come to believe to anyone who will listen, often in a not-so-subtle attempt to enroll them in your newfound belief system.

Those affected by "holy man's disease" would like everyone in their lives to come into agreement with their views and acknowledge them for their spiritual superiority. This ailment is exemplified by neophytes pretending to know all, even though they have yet to actualize their knowledge into wisdom via the experience of awakening. Essentially, the hallmark of holy man's disease is making the mistake of thinking that because you know something conceptually, you really *know* it, rather than realizing that true *knowing* can only come through direct experience.

Further, because of the ego's addiction to perfection, it's easy for the false self (ego) to masquerade as special, when in reality the enlightened path is accepting ordinariness—our humanness.

8. The Challenge of Spiritual Bypass

Like holy man's disease, this challenge usually happens at the early stages of awakening. It's a form of denial of unresolved issues by claiming a level of mastery that's yet to be achieved. Spiritual bypass often occurs through adopting the belief that it's not okay to have feelings. One draws the conclusion that negative emotions are not spiritual, and responds by bypassing these feelings rather than resolving them. This results in the spouting of spiritual principles that do not ring true but rather resound as empty platitudes. In other words, one mistakenly believes oneself further along than one is.

This challenge always reminds us of the story about a man who, in his quest for enlightenment, left his village and went up into the hills to meditate and quiet his mind. After 20 years, he perceived himself enlightened and, being good-hearted, came down from his cave to share his wisdom with others. As he was strolling back toward his village, he encountered a man walking in his direction. They greeted each other, and the second man said, "I remember you. You went away about 20 years ago. Where have you been?"

"I've been up in the mountains," the first man responded. "I've spent the last 20 years in deep meditation, and I've quieted my mind and am at peace."

"That sounds wonderful. I'd sure like to be at peace. What's it like?"

"It's wonderful. For one thing, I never get angry."

"That's amazing. You never get angry?"

"No, I never get angry, not at anything."

"Are you sure you never get angry?"

"Damn it! I said I never get angry, didn't I?"

As the preceding fable humorously portrays, it's easy to stumble into potholes along the spiritual path.

As a recap, here are the more common challenges of awakening:

1. *The Challenge of Cognitive Dissonance*

2. *The Challenge of Surrendering the Illusion of Control*

3. *The Challenge of Freedom from Identification with Roles and Personal History*

4. *The Challenge of Continuing to Participate*

5. *The Challenge of the Inadequacy of Words*

6. *The Challenge of Speed and Noise*

7. *The Challenge of Holy Man's Disease*

8. *The Challenge of Spiritual Bypass*

Meeting the Challenges Effectively

All of the aforementioned challenges present themselves as obstacles to continuing with the awakening process. And the way they all operate is through the dynamic of fear. As it dawns on you that there's an entirely different reality, which apparently contains the one you've been accustomed to thinking of as the *only* reality, it's not uncommon to fall into a deep-seated *fear of the unknown.*

But not to worry. You can use the wise counsel that don Juan gave Carlos Castaneda regarding the way through fear: "[A man] must not run away. He must defy his fear, and in spite of it he must take the next step in learning, and the next, and the next. He must be fully afraid, and yet he must not stop. That is the rule!" Fear is based upon the perception of an imagined future catastrophe resulting from doing what you are afraid of doing. By actually *doing* whatever you're afraid of doing, you can learn through experience that the imagined catastrophe doesn't happen, so you proceed with less and less fear. You come to understand that the awakening process is a continuous journey of one awareness after another, each building upon the wisdom of the last. If you simply hold a clear intention to wake up in accordance with the highest good, and not allow fear to stop you, you will continue to progress.

Individuals often ask us what qualities they can develop to assist them in their endeavors to overcome the challenges we just described and grow spiritually. Our answer is: *reverence, willingness, humility, perseverance, self-compassion, clear intention,* and *great courage.* In particular, we mean:

- *Reverence* for the great mystery of life itself, and its possibilities

- *Willingness* to question basic assumptions about what's true, because much of what people have learned while growing up is either not true at all, partially true, or seriously distorted

- *Humility* to bear in mind that no human being is in control

- *Perseverance* to hang in there when some of the more difficult patterns of negativity are surfacing

- *Self-compassion* for our humanness as we all proceed through the arduous process of awakening and living an ever more conscious life
- *Clear intention* to continue awakening
- *Great courage* to face the fear that accompanies awakening

The Blessings of Awakening

While the challenges to awakening are considerable, the benefits and blessings are well worth the effort. If we had to sum up the process itself, we'd say that it involves an upward shift in awareness such that individuals find themselves to be functioning in an expanded state of consciousness. This state has certain recognizable characteristics that include:

1. *Clarity.* Your perceptions tend to have been brought into focus. You know you're seeing things more clearly, and you begin to understand what in the East has been called *maya,* or illusion. As you learn to see past the illusions, you realize that there is much more meaning and purpose to life than you were previously aware of. The door to the dimension of spiritual reality opens as the distortions and misunderstandings that cloud the lens of perception dissolve. As Emerson said, "People only see what they are prepared to see."

2. *Acceptance.* You become aware that less and less disturbs your peace. There's an underlying sense of calm, even though nothing has changed outwardly. You're much less prone to judgment, "againstness," and "positionality"; and more willing to respond to life with neutrality. You begin to recognize others as Divine Beings, and the situations and circumstances of your life as learning devices.

3. *Joy and good humor.* You experience yourself as much more available to laughter. You realize that joy is not dependent upon external events, but is rather an inner state always present and

available. As the philosopher Pierre Teilhard de Chardin said, "Joy is the most infallible sign of the presence of God."

4. *Compassion.* As you look out at the world, you recognize that there are those who are suffering. You also recognize that you have a choice as to whether or not, and to what degree, you participate in assisting them. Regardless of whether you choose to respond outwardly, you can respond inwardly with an open heart and without judgment. As Buddha put it, "In separateness lies the world's great misery; in compassion lies the world's true strength."

5. *Love.* The most profound awareness is the self-evident presence of Love. It's no coincidence why accounts, both written and verbally reported, by the saints and mystics seem to be strangely similar. They were all talking about the same experience. And if you were to distill what they all described down to its essence, you would find that they expressed a sentiment that sages have been saying for ages and Dr. Hunter said those many years ago. It's worth repeating:

The nature of God is Love!

A Stunning Discovery

When contemplating the above principle, it doesn't take long for a fourth principle to sink in as it flows directly from the first three:

> ***Principle #4:*** *Since we are all part of God, our nature is*
> *also Love, and we have the opportunity to know our*
> *Loving nature experientially, here and now!*

If we are all part of God and our very nature is Love, then everything else in creation is also part of God, and it is all connected—much like an individual drop of water is a part of the ocean.

Further, directly following from this principle, it becomes clear that self-worth and a sense of value—commodities you have been striving so hard to earn because of an unconscious fear and guilt that you've done something wrong—are nothing but mental constructs that have no meaning. You are valuable simply because you are Divine. Worth and value are inherent and cannot, and need not, be earned. They are intrinsic to your being. You will see that the idea of needing to earn worth and value is about as irrelevant as needing to earn the air you breathe. What will be of primary interest to you is growing spiritually while at the same time living your life fully in ways that have heart, meaning, and purpose. These realizations and the blessings that flow naturally from them are uplifting and will fill you with great gratitude.

It is from our personal experience of assisting many people in their quest for greater Self-awareness over the years that we say, without a doubt: *Waking up is not so hard. In fact, it's our future, our destiny, and the purpose of our life on this planet. We will all awaken eventually. The only question is when.*

Let's Start Practicing

At about this stage of inquiry, people usually ask if there are practices that can assist them in moving into a greater awareness of spiritual reality. As a matter of fact, there are several simple yet profound attitudes and skills you can begin using immediately. They are designed to assist you in having the experience of what *Seeing Through Soul-Centered Eyes* is all about. We'll share the most essential one with you here. It's based on the principle introduced earlier, that the nature of God is Love, which is our innermost nature as well. The skill is composed of two parts:

Seeing the Loving Essence

The first is attitudinal, a way of being, and can be practiced all by itself. We call it *Seeing the Loving Essence,* which is the practice of seeing yourself and others through the eyes of Loving. It involves moving into a frame of reference where you begin seeing everyone as a Divine Being having a human experience regardless of what's going on in the individual's physical-world reality or between the two of you. This is a conscious, intentional practice of the essential message contained in the beautiful Hindu greeting, *Namaste,* which means: "I bow to the Divinity inherent in you. The Soul within me recognizes, acknowledges, respects, and appreciates the Soul within you; for in reality, we are one—we are both drops within the same ocean."

Imagine meeting everyone you encounter with a Namaste attitude of respect for their spiritual nature—with no exceptions. It would apply equally to your best friend and your worst enemy. In fact, if you'd care to experience a remarkable upward shift in consciousness, we suggest you experiment by looking at each and every person you meet (as well as yourself) through the Soul-Centered Eyes of Namaste for this next week and see what happens. Consciously look for their Loving Essence. You just may find your entire way of being with people changing. And a really good idea is to write about your experiences that result from adopting this attitude in your journal.

Heart-Centered Listening

We refer to the second part of this skill as *Heart-Centered Listening.* As professional counselors for more years than we'd like to admit, we've mediated thousands of conversations, especially between couples. And there is no doubt that one of the biggest challenges people have is truly listening to, and hearing, one another.

Many people think they're good listeners, but few actually are. Part of the challenge with effective listening is that messages are sent and received at four distinct levels:

1. The most obvious level—and the one most people focus on when they think of listening—is *content.* You may believe you have mastered listening when you can parrot back what the other person has said, thus demonstrating that you've heard them. Actually, content accounts for a relatively small portion of most communication, and it's open to interpretation depending upon what each individual perceives as important.

2. Next, there's *tonality,* or how something is said. Most people will remember *how* something was said long after they have forgotten *what* was said. Tonality can be thought of as the energy upon which a communication rides.

3. Then there's listening to the *person,* which is quite independent of the content being shared. This is where really good listeners excel. Listening to the person means deeply perceiving and receiving the person who is sharing. It involves listening with the conscious attitude of Namaste or Seeing the Loving Essence. As St. Benedict said: "Listen and attend with the ear of your heart." If you are in a conversation with a really good listener, you will come away from it feeling that you truly have been seen and heard.

4. The fourth level of listening occurs at the level of *meanings.* This involves hearing not only the content but the deeper meaning behind the content. This skill poses and answers the question: *What is the essential message this person is sharing?*

Individuals may be expressing a need, a perception, or a desire. When you're listening on this fourth level, you're looking to see what their communication really represents to them beyond their words. What are they trying to get across to you either directly or indirectly? For instance, a spouse may be saying, "You don't listen to me," but what he or she is truly attempting to communicate is: "Please listen to me."

Really good communicators know that they will be much more effective if they focus on listening to another rather than getting their point of view across. If you want to have deeper, more meaningful relationships, develop your listening skills. People yearn to be truly heard, to be received. At its finest, Heart-Centered Listening is an experience of Acceptance, Communion, and Oneness; for when a person feels heard, he or she also feels loved.

We recommend setting the following intention when listening to another: *My intention is to honor who you are and listen not only* *to <u>what</u> you say, but also to catch the deeper levels of <u>what you mean.</u> I know I will learn the most about you by listening to your points of view while centering my awareness in my heart and giving you my complete attention.*

Soul-Centered Practices

Seeing the Loving Essence and Heart-Centered Listening

Here's how to use *Heart-Centered Listening*—within the context of an attitude of *Seeing the Loving Essence*—in your next communication:

1. Center your awareness in your heart and consciously look for the Loving Essence in the person in your presence. By doing so, you're signifying your respect for the Soul before you, regardless of who the person is, his or her situation or circumstances, or the nature of your relationship.

2. Maintain awareness that you're in conversation with another Divine Being who is engaged in having a human experience. Remember that as a Soul, the other person has all the inner resources necessary to effectively respond to his or her situation.

3. Set your intention to open yourself to look with the eyes of your heart and listen with the ears of your heart.

4. Give the person before you your full attention, your respect, and your caring. (No meaningful conversation is ever going to occur while the TV is on.)

5. Follow his or her lead. Listen at all four levels: *content, tonality,* to the *person,* and for his or her *meaning.*

6. Assist the other person in giving dimension and depth to what is shared through the use of minimal encouragement such as, "I really hear you. Would you like to say a bit more about that?"

7. Support the individual in completing one topic before going on to the next. The more information people share at one time, the more difficult it can be to follow them and effectively respond to all that they're saying.

8. Resist the urge to give advice. You are engaging in *Seeing the Loving Essence* and *Heart-Centered Listening!*

If you're wondering how such a simple listening skill might make a difference, we'd like to share the following account. It relates the experience of a former student who was part of a seven-woman contingent of USM graduates who journeyed to the Dead Sea near Amman, Jordan, to facilitate a workshop that was part of the Partnership for Peace Program called "Towards Justice and Reconciliation." This event, which took place in 2004, was sponsored by the United Nations and included approximately 50 Israeli and 50 Palestinian professional women. Due to political tensions, the conference could not be held in either Israel or Palestine, so these courageous women made their way to neutral Jordan for three days to explore specific initiatives that aimed to improve the environment for building peace by encouraging dialogue and promoting understanding.

The workshop was called Dialogue Skills for Influencing Change, and consisted largely of three-person processes during which one person was the Listener, one was the Sharer, and the third served as what we call a Neutral Observer. The Sharer was invited to speak about something personally meaningful and relevant to the intention of the conference. The Listener was not to comment on what the Sharer said, but rather to simply practice the skill the trio was seeking to learn, which, in this case, was Heart-Centered Listening. The Neutral Observer's task was to silently hold a safe and accepting space for both Sharer and Listener, and then to provide constructive feedback to both of them regarding their effectiveness in practicing the skill.

Here is our graduate's account:

On the second day of the workshop, the women began to trickle in. I noticed as the two most influential women in the workshop, one Palestinian and one Israeli, both of whom happened to be psychiatrists, arrived. I was asked to be their Neutral Observer.

As the exercise began, I was a bit nervous about being with the Palestinian psychiatrist in particular. She was young, militant, angry, and appeared to be quite outspoken. During the previous day, she had stood to aggressively share her grievances. She came to express her position to the Israelis, and had not given an opening to move into any form of resolution of the issues. (It just so happens that my father is a psychiatrist. Spirit is pretty funny!)

The women were instructed on the exercise, and despite the structure of the process, immediately began debating. It was as if the two countries were airing their grievances and animosities rather than two women simply talking together. I interrupted several times, suggesting that they work with the skill of Heart-Centered Listening to see what might happen. I must have intervened four times, as their exchange was escalating. These were two highly educated, intelligent, and experienced women who were talking with great passion. You can imagine the fire that was moving through them.

Then the Israeli psychiatrist "got it." She stopped reacting and began listening. It was remarkable. As she held the space for the Palestinian psychiatrist, they both began to relax and became more centered within themselves. I could sense their countries' histories fall away as they began genuinely listening to each other, woman to woman. The authenticity of their exchange was deeply moving to witness.

During post-process large-group sharing, the Israeli psychiatrist shared with the group that she realized after all these years as a psychiatrist in private practice, working in hospitals, and teaching at a university, that she had *never truly listened*. (She told me afterward that she realized that up until then when she listened to people, she was usually just waiting to tell them how they were wrong.) I felt this was an incredible insight that demonstrated the power of a one-hour dialogue to begin transforming a lifelong pattern. That she felt safe enough to share it with the entire group was nothing short of miraculous.

This woman said that in the trio she realized that although she considered herself quite liberal, that wasn't enough. She recognized that there were far deeper issues for the Palestinian people than she had previously understood or realized. She also shared that she actually felt frustrated that she couldn't do more to bring peace to the region. This was a profound moment for her, and we were blessed to witness the shift in her consciousness.

Then the Palestinian psychiatrist stood to share her experience with the group. This time, she was considerably softer. She stood without the defiance and anger that had been her previous persona, and shared with tears in her eyes that this was the first time in her life that she had ever felt heard. She said, "It was truly a profound encounter. Not only did I experience being heard, I listened with acceptance to an Israeli and heard that her concerns are similar to mine. I was truly surprised."

The two women experienced a deep connection with each other and chose to continue their dialogue during lunch. Clearly, they had fulfilled the UN's hope of participants moving beyond a competition of lamentations rooted in ancient resentments and animosities into a dialogue where, at least for these women, peace truly prevailed.

This experience was most inspirational for me. I remember it as if it happened yesterday, and I suspect I will remember it for the rest of my life. What an affirmation of the power of Heart-Centered Listening.

Here's a fabulous quote from contemporary author Brenda Ueland that communicates the magic of deeply listening to another:

> Listening is a magnetic and strange thing, a creative force. . . . [When] people really listen to us, with quiet fascinated attention, that the little fountain begins to work again, to accelerate in the most surprising way.

In our experience, what Brenda has written is absolutely accurate. Happy *Heart-Centered Listening!*

∽∽

Stem Sentences to Write and Contemplate

- If the nature of God is Love, then . . .
- If the nature of my Soul is Love, then . . .
- I can practice *Seeing the Loving Essence* when . . .
- I can practice *Heart-Centered Listening* when . . .

Repeat as often as necessary.

CHAPTER THREE

LIFE IS FOR LEARNING

We're all learning to use the external world as a feedback mechanism to guide us into the Sacred.

Mary and I are fortunate in that we've always treasured the process of learning. So it's not surprising that we would meet on a university campus and then go on to launch USM together. One of the things we've observed over the years is this: a primary obstacle to some people moving forward in any given area of their lives is that they simply don't choose to take time to learn about the dimension within which they would like to progress. To us, one of the real challenges many face today is that life has become so fast paced that cultivating a meaningful practice of inward inquiry is rendered more and more difficult when instant gratification, sound bites, and superficiality are the norm.

At USM, we establish the context of what we call a *Learning Orientation to Life.* One of the most important, fundamental aspects within this context has to do with how life is experienced by an awakening individual. In this frame of reference, we assist people in learning the dynamics of how consciousness functions. We do this because it's significantly easier to navigate the unfamiliar waters of awakening when one understands the nature of the "sea" upon which one is sailing.

As spiritual as we may all aspire to be, it's imperative to remember that we're also living in a physical-world reality. Thus, for people consciously interested in spiritual progression, there are two distinctly different contexts and skills we must consider—one for spiritual reality and another for physical-world reality.

Fortunately, growing spiritually doesn't require you to divest yourself of worldly possessions and become a monk. In fact, it's essential that you work within the context of the physical-world reality in which you find yourself. In this regard, learning how to use everyday experience as the grist for your spiritual mill is fundamental. Within a spiritual context, every thought and action is filled with spiritual opportunity.

Dag Hammarskjöld, former secretary-general of the United Nations, seems to have had it right when he said, "In our era, the road to holiness necessarily passes through the world of action." Indeed, we appear to have reached a unique period of time and circumstance in human history.

The Goal Line of Life

Let's start with learning in physical-world reality, or what we at USM refer to as the *Goal Line of Life*. Positive movement in this reality occurs as follows:

Figure 1

NEGATIVE EXPERIENCE ⟶ **POSITIVE EXPERIENCE**

GOAL LINE
Success in the Material World

For most people, the above diagram represents their basic approach to life, with success defined as moving from negative experience toward more positive experience. Gains on the Goal Line are frequently measured in financial units, and may also extend into less tangible areas such as relationships, health, creative expression, and so on. Because of the nature of the physical world, movement on the Goal Line is external. It happens "out there," and is usually readily observable by others. In fact, judging by the number of self-help programs promising to fulfill all of one's "heartfelt desires," a casual observer could easily conclude that such achievement represents the highest form of human fulfillment. Actually, nothing could be further from the truth. What's seldom recognized is that such success is temporary. Consider the following:

1. *Everything you acquire in the material world will need to be maintained.*

2. *You cannot create beyond what's permitted by your spiritual curriculum.*

3. *When you are all done creating, you will not be any happier than when you started.*

4. *In order to awaken to your next steps spiritually, you must be willing to surrender anything you've previously created.*

What are we saying? Nothing less than this: true happiness is not to be found along life's Goal Line. While you can experience temporary highs, you can never discover who you are, your purpose in life, and how you can make a meaningful contribution in your world through success on the Goal Line. One of the wealthiest men we know spends a significant number of his waking hours considering how he can assist others. That's true wealth, and it's to be found in a dimension beyond the Goal Line.

Life's Learning Line

When those who are ready dare to journey beyond the Goal Line, they enter a dimension largely unknown. They pass through the ancient yet modern portal marked SPIRITUAL EVOLUTION. To navigate this territory, a completely different context of reality or road map is required because the nature of this terrain can only be referenced experientially and doesn't lend itself to external measures.

Spiritual evolution happens *within*. It's composed of inner experiences not readily observable externally. It's not subject to publicly verifiable validation, although others may see the results, as demonstrated in certain changes in one's behavior, attitude, and way of being.

Further, there is no direct correlation between spiritual growth and gains on the Goal Line. If this were not so, the wealthier a person was, the more spiritual he or she would be; and by extension, billionaires would be saints. Actually, the two dimensions are completely independent, as depicted in the following illustration.

Figure 2

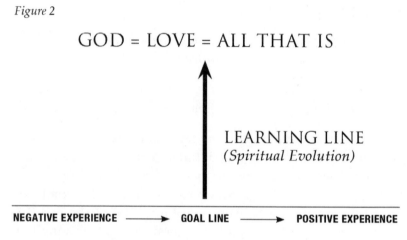

GOD = LOVE = ALL THAT IS

LEARNING LINE
(Spiritual Evolution)

NEGATIVE EXPERIENCE ⟶ GOAL LINE ⟶ POSITIVE EXPERIENCE

Success in the Material World

To distinguish between the two contexts, we refer to the dimension of spiritual evolution as the *Learning Line of Life*. The Learning Line is about the degree to which you are learning to be more Loving and Compassionate and are functioning more consciously within parameters of the reality of spirit as determined by the *nature* of spirit, which is Love. The Learning Line has nothing to do with whether or not you actually achieve your worldly goals. Thus, we have arrived at the fifth major principle of what life looks like in the context of Spiritual Psychology when *Seeing Through Soul-Centered Eyes:*

Principle #5: *Physical-world reality exists for the purpose of spiritual evolution.*

For most of the world's population, this is a meaningless principle. If you asked the majority of people about the nature of the earth, they would probably say something like: "The physical world is a planet called Earth, one of billions that exists in physical reality, which is the only reality there is. Our job is to study the earth scientifically and gain control over the forces of nature. At best, life is a struggle, and the goal is to survive and be as successful as we can. The more successful we are, the better."

However, from the vantage point of the Learning Line, Souls come to Earth to learn, and there appear to be many different classrooms going on simultaneously. Some are learning how to fulfill basic survival needs; while others are learning about families, boundaries, responsibilities, communities, and much more. Some are learning about creative expression, and some about service and altruism. And there are those Souls who are completing everything this particular learning opportunity has to offer . . . you might even say they are *graduating.* They've grown beyond the apparent dualities of *right* and *wrong* and are centered in a place of Acceptance, Loving, and Compassion. There is nothing more for them to learn here.

Spiritual Curriculum Everywhere

This lesson was brought home to me rather vividly one day as I was walking with Dr. Hunter in downtown Alamogordo. We were on our way to visit someone in the hospital when a young man being pushed in a wheelchair approached. He didn't seem very "present" and had little control over his body's contortions. I didn't know the nature of his physical condition, and I found myself feeling sorry for this person.

As we passed him, Dr. Hunter noticed my discomfort and said, "The reason you feel the way you do about that young man is because you don't know his spiritual curriculum. If you could *see* clearly, you would see that this is his last lifetime on Earth. He has learned all there is to learn here, and this physical limitation is his final test. He will pass it simply by enduring his condition for the rest of his life. He's really quite happy, because he knows this. It's a very beautiful thing."

She was right. My pity was self-referenced. I imagined how awful it would be if I were in that man's situation. I'd assumed that my standard of outer physical reality was all there was. What did I know about what his Soul was completing through this experience? Dr. Hunter, on the other hand, was seeing *spiritually,* and from her point of view the young man's lesson and blessing were revealed.

Seeing from within the spiritual context, you observe that all of life's experiences are part of each Soul's unique curriculum. It's wise to approach physical-world reality with a healthy respect and a Learning Orientation, regardless of how any particular situation may appear.

In fact, one way you might assess how you're doing with your own spiritual curriculum is to think about a challenging situation you went through recently. Then think about how you probably would have handled, or actually did handle, that same circumstance a year ago. If you notice a positive difference, meaning that you recently managed it with more Love and Compassion than you did in the past, that difference is an excellent—although not physically quantifiable—indicator of your spiritual growth.

For example, a recent USM student shared that she had resented her ex-husband for years because he didn't pay for their daughter's college tuition even though he had promised to do so. After considerable healing work centering around her former partner, she eventually moved into a place of inner freedom. She was then able to attend her daughter's graduation and sit next to her ex-husband with feelings of Love and Gratitude for the part he had played in both her life and her daughter's. The resentment was gone.

She later shared the following in class: "I finally got free of using my ex-husband as my 'ex-cuse' for my feelings of resentment." The shift in her attitude that had resulted from her releasing the inner disturbance was a clear indicator of her growth over the year. She was *seeing* things differently.

From within a spiritual context, you perceive a remarkable awareness. You see that Earth is perfect just the way it is—a magnificent learning environment for spiritual evolution. You also observe your earthly existence as providing countless situations and circumstances that are perfect learning opportunities. With this understanding, you can begin to make better use of those you've provided for yourself in service to spiritual awakening. There are no mistakes and no failures in Spirit. There are only an infinite number of ongoing learning opportunities. It's like the movie *Groundhog Day,* where Bill Murray relived the same day over and over again until he transformed. And then, miraculously, his life also changed.

Pretty much everyone has been taught that you can't take it with you. Depending upon what is meant by "it," that statement may or may not be true. If "it" refers to homes and cars and lifestyles, we would agree. But if "it" refers to the individual learning garnered while here on Earth, that's another story.

Consider the possibility that gains on the Learning Line are precisely what you take with you when you pass from this world and are precisely what's meant by spiritual evolution. Of course, it's up to each person which line you choose to spend the bulk of your time pursuing.

Personally, we see no reason why you can't be actively involved on both the Goal and Learning Lines in a balanced way, as long as a clear sight of the relative and ultimate value of each is maintained. In fact, when *seen* through the lens of Spiritual Psychology, there's a dynamic interplay between the two, such that challenges on the Goal Line are recognized and properly utilized as opportunities, and even blessings, on the Learning Line.

The trick for most people is learning to see life through *learning-oriented,* as well as *goal-oriented,* eyes. It is possible to master the skills of worldly success as seen through the ego-centered lens of duality and also choose to see through Soul-Centered Eyes . . . to see the perfection inherent in all of life's vicissitudes.

Here's John Keats's description of the process:

> I will call the *world* a School instituted for the purpose of teaching little children to read—I will call the *human heart* the *horn Book* used in that School—and I will call the *Child able to read, the Soul* made from that *School* and its *hornbook.* Do you not see how necessary a World of Pains and troubles is to school an Intelligence and make it a soul? A Place where the heart must feel and suffer in a thousand diverse ways! Not merely is the Heart a hornbook. It is the Mind's Bible. . . .

As Souls, we are aware that we're all here fulfilling a spiritual purpose, or we wouldn't be here at all. The opportunity is to discover how to use the Goal Line as a jumping-off place for gains on the Learning Line rather than only for Goal Line gains as ends in and of themselves.

Growing spiritually is about focusing more on the Learning Line while living in a world that appears to have gone overboard on the Goal Line. As Dr. Hunter pointed out, "We all exist in both the spiritual and physical worlds simultaneously while we're here on Earth. We have one foot in each camp, whether we know it or not, and this situation provides us with a unique combination of favorable circumstances for spiritual growth. It's no accident that we find ourselves here. There is spiritual opportunity everywhere as soon as we open our eyes to perceive it."

Discovering Another Way

What does it look like to be aware of and utilize experience for purposes of growth on both the Goal and Learning Lines of life?

As I said at the beginning of this chapter, Mary and I are fortunate in that we've always treasured the process of learning. So it's not surprising that we love to meet people whose lives are a labor of love, and being around them reinforces the value of a Learning Orientation to Life. We've noticed four attributes of such individuals:

- They appear to have boundless energy.
- They love to learn.

- They have tremendous love and enthusiasm for their chosen endeavor.
- They appear motivated by something other than material success.

Being around such people reinforces the value of a Learning Orientation to Life, and I'd love to share one of my most significant memories of such experiences. So I invite you to come along on an adventure into my past that took me beyond the limitations of my conditioned thinking and into a reality I had no idea even existed.

The Adventure of Finding Water

As a young man, I spent a great deal of time in northern Vermont, where I owned a large three-story A-frame. I enjoyed skiing, so I used the house on weekends as a base for hitting the slopes with friends. When we'd head up there in the summer, our activities ranged from mountain motorcycling, hiking, and flying airplanes . . . to simply being in nature.

I also co-owned with my dad a parcel of 68 acres of gorgeous, undeveloped land. My plan was to build my ideal mountain retreat on it someday. Half of the property was full of beautiful northern pines, and the other half was pasture that we rented to a neighboring dairy farmer. He paid us a minimal amount, but what he did was far more valuable: he farmed the land, which kept it well maintained all year long.

One of the things this property did not have was a source of water. Now, in northern Vermont, if you drill into the ground just about anywhere, you'll eventually hit water. But *eventually* could mean down several hundred feet. With drilling costs measured in dollars per feet drilled, a landowner's goal was to find water as close to the surface as possible.

One day I was explaining my situation to an acquaintance in the local hardware store, and he recommended that I talk to Holly Greenslit. He admitted that Holly was an odd sort of fellow, but swore up and down that this guy could find water by using a forked stick cut from a witch hazel tree. Apparently, while unheard of in downtown New York City, such happenings were not at all unusual in rural areas such as this.

Holly was reputed to do more than just locate water. Evidently, he could also tell the water's depth, as well as the volume and direction of its flow. He apparently was even able to discern whether it was potable or contaminated.

That's where my predicament began. I'd always considered myself a pragmatic, scientific sort of guy. On the other hand, I did pride myself on having an open mind. After all, wasn't I also interested in parapsychology?

But finding water with a forked stick? Wasn't that the stuff of folktales? Was I really willing to put my money where my mouth was? I must admit that I did find the idea fascinating, and my saving grace was that I was sufficiently aware to know there was much that I didn't know. *Okay*, I told myself. *I'm in! If nothing else, I'll do it as an experiment just to see what will happen.*

Holly lived in the nearby town of Warren in a trailer. He had no car or phone and traveled everywhere by foot or single-speed bicycle. So if you wanted to make an appointment with Holly, you had to go to his trailer and do it in person, which I did.

He was a short man, who I guessed was in his 60s, and he'd spent most of his life in the Vermont woods working as a logger. He was a man of few words, and his face had an unusual quality to it: his eyes and mouth seemed to twinkle in harmony with each other. Here was a man who, to all outward appearances, was living in poverty; yet his very presence communicated complete comfort with his physical circumstances. It was as if he had a secret that may have been secret even to *him,* but its presence revealed itself in his smile. I liked him instantly.

When I explained my situation and where the property was located and asked if Holly would come, he said, "Sure." Demonstrating my New York upbringing, I asked what his charge would be.

"Whatever you'd like to pay me," was his reply.

"When can you come?"

"I'm free right now."

So we climbed into my four-wheel-drive vehicle, and off we went. When we arrived on the land, the first thing Holly did was go into the woods and cut a forked branch from a tree. He asked me where on the property I'd like to look for the water and then proceeded, stick held horizontal to the earth, walking lengthwise across the area I delineated. At several places the tip of his stick would violently jerk downward. He had me mark those places with a small stake driven into the ground.

When Holly was done, we went back over each of the marked spots once again. With his stick at the ready, he began asking himself a series of silent questions. He gave me the answers and asked me to write them down.

Afterward, we reviewed the data and chose a place that seemed to me, at least on the surface, no different from any other place within a hundred feet in any direction. We chose this particular spot because it was at the high point of the slope of the land and would be an excellent building site. By Holly's indications, this was also where a suitable source of water was only 11 feet from the surface.

What? Eleven feet? Considering several well drillers had previously estimated that we'd likely need to drill at least 200 feet to hit good water, this was an incredible prediction. If accurate, it also meant that a drilling rig wouldn't be required because 11 feet was just within the range of a common backhoe.

I drove Holly home, thanked him both personally and financially, for which he was grateful, and then considered what to do next. I wanted to believe him. But good drinking water at 11 feet—how believable was that, really?

I pondered this for a few days, and then I decided what to do. The well-conditioned adult scientist inside my head surrendered to the naïve, childlike mystic in my heart. I justified my choice by reasoning that since the cost of a backhoe and operator for a few hours wouldn't be all that much, why not go for it? After all, it was a kind of research experiment and, if nothing else, would be interesting.

So, a few days later, onto the land rumbled a bright yellow back-hoe. Holly had advised me about the direction to bring the machine in so its weight wouldn't crush the alleged underground water vein. I explained to the driver how I wanted him to position the rig.

"You been talking to Holly?" the operator asked.

"Yes." I sheepishly grinned. "Have you dug many holes behind his work?"

"Some," he said in a matter-of-fact Vermont sort of way. "Holly's right a lot of the time." And with the same nonchalance with which one would order a chicken-salad sandwich, he turned to his digging. I just love Vermonters.

Down we dug. I became more excited with each bucket of dirt. When we got down ten feet and were about to plunge in for the telltale scoop, I was psyched up for a geyser like Old Faithful in Yellowstone National Park.

It didn't happen. What did happen was that a tiny trace of water began seeping into the bottom of the hole.

"There's your water," the driver said, with no apparent aware-ness of the enormity of his simple statement. To me, he had uttered words equal in magnitude to the shouts when gold was first found at Sutter's Mill.

But where there should have been water by the gallon, there was only a trickle. I stared incredulously while my inner critic sneered, *That's it? That's what we've been waiting for? That's about enough water to float a mosquito.*

The backhoe operator interrupted my inner drama by asking when I wanted him to return to finish the job. Not knowing just what he meant, I said I would call him after I had talked it over with Holly. He agreed and suggested that he fill the hole about half full in the meantime so that it didn't fill up with water. I fought back the urge to keel over with laughter. It seemed to me that at the rate it was coming in, it would take about ten years for that hole to overflow. But I agreed regardless, and he proceeded to fill the hole.

I couldn't get to Holly's fast enough, but he wasn't home. Since I was much too excited to wait, I went looking for him. I found him about a mile out of town on the side of the road, his bicycle close by and a scythe in his hand. He was busily cutting the weeds that are always threatening to overrun Vermont's back roads in the middle of summer.

"Hi, Holly. What are you doing?"

"Paying my taxes," he replied.

"What?" I asked, laughing. "Really, how come you're cutting the weeds?"

"This is how I pay my town taxes. Since I don't have much in the way of money, I agreed to keep the weeds down a mile on each side of town as payment of my taxes."

A brief thought passed through my mind about how this approach might work midwinter in Manhattan with an army of tax-evading snow shovelers, but I quickly dismissed it. I excitedly shared what had happened on the land and asked his opinion about what to do next.

He leaned on his scythe in the way I imagined had been done for centuries but was seldom seen nowadays. "Now that we know the water's there, you need to order a piece of aluminum culvert pipe 15 or 16 feet long and 3 feet wide. You'll want a concrete cap for it, three cinder blocks, and a yard of rough gravel. You'll also need to get a small pitcher pump with 15 feet of pipe to attach to it."

I wrote feverishly as he continued, "Once you've got all the materials, you'll need to get the backhoe to come again and dig out the hole so you can put the culvert on its end down into the hole. That will be your well."

Little did I realize at the time that I had entered the wild and wonderful world of *dowsing*. It turned out that knowing how to place a well into a hole filled with water is every bit as important as finding the water in the first place. I had a lot to learn.

Holly taught me that the loose gravel goes in first so that the underground vein is free to flow through it unimpeded. Then the three cinder blocks are laid in with the spaces in the blocks horizontal to the ground so the water can flow through them. Once leveled, they form a flat tripod base upon which the culvert rests like an enormous inverted aluminum cigar. Without the gravel and blocks, the weight of the culvert itself would shortly block off the underground vein, which would simply "learn" to flow around it. Amazing!

Several days later, under Holly's watchful eye, we put the culvert in place. It came up above ground level by about six feet, so we had the backhoe driver build a slight mound with the leftover dirt so that we could walk up onto it. The concrete cap then sat at waist level.

As I looked down into the hole, I didn't see a thing. Holly noticed my doubt and simply said, "Nothing to do until tomorrow when we take a sample to send off to the university for a potability test—to see if it's good for drinking."

When we returned the following day, Holly helped me lift the heavy concrete cap off the now-upright end of the culvert so we could see inside. I was stunned! The water level had risen to within six feet of the cap. The culvert now had a water supply in it that was three feet wide by about nine feet deep. As I stood there contemplating what had happened, amazement gave way to sheer astonishment and then awe! And just as Holly had predicted, the potability test came back positive. It was excellent drinking water.

Endless Possibilities

That summer, I spent a considerable amount of time with Holly. We made a deal: he would teach me to dowse, assuming I had the ability, and in return I would drive him to and from his dowsing jobs.

It turned out that I did have the ability, and true to his word, Holly taught me how to do it. When he got a call, I would drive him to the place, and he would have me dowse it first and mark my findings. Then he would come behind me to check it out. I must admit my biggest frustration was that even though I could dowse, my markings were off course as often as on course. Holly reassured me that I only lacked experience.

I recall one day in particular when I couldn't get any dowsing markings on target. Holly gave me his little smile and said, "You know, people will often tell you that all you need is talent to be good at something. It's not true. Talent is only the first step. There are many talented people who are not very good at applying their gift. If you really want to be good at something, what you must do is practice and gain experience in developing your talent. The more you practice, the more accurate your marking will become. I've spent over 40 years dowsing, and I'm still not accurate 100 percent of the time."

Then he said something extraordinary: "You know, dowsing is the kind of thing you can track and measure to see how you're progressing, which is what you've been doing. You feel good when your results are good and bad when your results are bad, like today. But what's most valuable in life isn't measurable. How do you measure the quality of the experience we're having when we're dowsing? How do you measure the beauty of a sunset? And even if you come up with a way, will your measurements add up to the experience of watching one? If you spend less time measuring and more time appreciating, you'll be much better off in the long run."

I've never forgotten that piece of wisdom Holly shared with me, and much later his words found expression in our next principle of *Seeing Through Soul-Centered Eyes*:

Principle #6: Spiritual evolution (growth) is a process, not an event.

In addition to being Holly's student, I learned a lot about dowsing by reading. From everything I could find, I surmised that the use of a "witching stick" (dowsing rod)—or anything else for that matter—was simply the dowser's way of giving himself permission to utilize some form of sixth sense or intuitive ability. I suggested to Holly that his dowsing abilities might not necessarily be limited to finding water.

Holly was as open as I was, and together we developed a protocol for him to use in diagnosing lawn mowers, as repairing them was one of the ways he earned money. I suggested he try to dowse, rather than physically test, them to assess the mechanical problems. In theory, this approach would cut down his turnaround time considerably. And darned if it didn't work!

Above all, I loved going into the woods with Holly. His knowledge of the forest was enormous. He knew about mushrooms, roots, and tree bark. He knew which plants were edible and inedible, and which could be used to make teas for different purposes. My favorite was tea from the bark of a cherry tree. It didn't seem to have any practical or medicinal use, but I just loved the way it tasted.

Once, after he'd gotten to a place inside himself where he trusted me, Holly said, "Come with me to the back of the trailer. I want to show you something." He had used the woods behind his trailer many times to help me practice my dowsing skill, and by now we both knew every water source for hundreds of feet around.

"Watch this," he declared, and began walking, eyes closed and hands outstretched, as if he were hugging an invisible person, only with his palms turned down. As he walked over a place where I knew an underground vein to be, his hands would vibrate violently. "I don't really need the stick," he admitted. "But when I don't use it, I notice that people get really nervous."

✑✑

My time with Holly resulted in his teaching me a great deal about dowsing. It included learning about how to walk through a field looking for water, how to approach and dig a hole for a well, how to build a well so that the water would continue to flow into it, and how to dowse for other things as well.

It was largely Goal Line learning insofar as the art of dowsing was concerned, and it could have ended there, but it didn't. More important in the long run were all my Learning Line lessons. I came to understand how a person can be happy with relatively little in the way of material possessions. I learned how to be in the woods and appreciate nature in ways I could never have imagined from my New York City upbringing. And I experienced continual pleasure and amazement while learning new things, like dowsing for lawn-mower malfunctions. Most of all, I was able to grasp the importance of maintaining an open mind and cultivating a willingness to surrender old ways of thinking and being in the world. I learned how essential it is to be willing to let go of anything I think I know in service to discovering something I don't know—even the possibility of becoming aware of new senses, like the ability to dowse.

I loved Holly, and although he died several years ago, I treasure the lessons he taught me to this day. Probably the most important of these is that all of life is for learning. Today's new experience will be the foundation upon which tomorrow's opportunity will reveal itself. And tomorrow I'll have more appreciation for that new opportunity than I have today, because I will be a different person. Thus, our seventh principle:

Principle #7: All of life is for Learning.

With this principle as an intention, the opportunity presents itself to everyone to be a wiser and more loving person tomorrow, assuming that today's experiences are utilized to grow in one's capacity for Compassion and Love. What a thought, to realize that we're blessed—as we *all* are—with abundant learning opportunities every single day if we have the wit to use the events of our lives in that way.

For Holly, everything was a new adventure. After I helped him learn how to diagnose lawn mowers, every time we got together he'd start out by asking me what I'd read since we last met. I realized that we had in common a deep desire to learn and to not allow preconceptions or reservations to stop our inquiry.

And if we're all here to learn and grow, it's extremely useful to assume what's been called a *beginner's mind* and to question our most basic assumptions about everything. In order to learn, it's essential to admit that we don't know, for it's only when we acknowledge that we truly don't know that we have any chance of learning something new. The more we can enter into a Learning Orientation to Life, the more we learn how to flow with our Souls' purpose, and the more we'll experience Peace and Loving, which are our natural birthright.

∽∽

Stem Sentences to Write Down and Contemplate

- In my life, the Goal Line includes . . .
- In my life, the Learning Line includes . . .
- If physical-world reality exists for the purpose of spiritual evolution, then . . .
- If all of life is for Learning, then . . .
- If the endgame isn't success on the Goal Line, then . . .
- An opportunity for me on the Learning Line is . . .

Repeat as often as necessary.

CHAPTER FOUR

CONSCIOUSNESS IN A NUTSHELL

Wins on the Goal Line stay here, while wins on the Learning Line go with you. It's the Learning Line that leads Home to God and where progress in spiritual evolution is made.

If life is primarily for learning, and if the physical world exists for the purpose of spiritual advancement, where do you go from here? What exactly are you here to learn, and how can Spiritual Psychology assist you in advancing spiritually?

These are valid questions. One metaphor that has been used to describe this situation is that of lighting up the darkness. In this context, the question becomes: "Can you please tell me where to get a well-functioning lamp?"

Motivational speaker and author John Bradshaw once offered this clue:

> A lot of people jump into higher consciousness and forget about lower consciousness. They haven't done their ego work, their feeling work. They are blissed out. It's just another mood alteration and it's a hell of a trip. I did it myself. I was into Shamanism, energy healing, spirit canoes, the whole trip. It became very important for me to realize all of that was a kind of intellectual defense. A wonderful mood-alteration—compulsive spirituality. It was a way to stay out of my feelings. I think all that stuff is really valid, but if you don't do your ego work, what I call the original pain work, it will pull you back.

Our years of experience bear out Bradshaw's admonition that ". . . if you don't do your ego work, what I call the original pain work, it will pull you back." But just what is "ego work," or "original pain work," and why is it so important? And, assuming it is important, how do you effectively do it?

For many people, life has little meaning in and of itself, and is just something to get through with the least possible pain and suffering. It's the position of Macbeth when he utters the words that Shakespeare wrote:

> *And all our yesterdays have lighted fools*
> *The way to dusty death. Out, out, brief candle!*
> *Life's but a walking shadow, a poor player*
> *That struts and frets his hour upon the stage*
> *And then is heard no more. It is a tale*
> *Told by an idiot, full of sound and fury,*
> *Signifying nothing.*

Not the most uplifting message, to be sure. But once you become aware of the possibility of spiritual reality, you begin to entertain a different perspective. You begin to realize that you can still "strut and fret" your hour upon the stage, only now you can do so with an agenda. You become aware of your spiritual curriculum and the opportunities available to you for spiritual growth. Life as a "walking shadow" upon a stage where you, the "poor player," live out your own drama sounds like a pretty accurate description of Goal Line living. And there's a different *play* being enacted on the Learning Line. Here, life is a tale told by a Soul, full of Peace and Love, signifying everything.

As has been previously indicated, one of the ironies of awakening and continuing to progress spiritually is that it's mostly an unlearning process. You must learn how to unlearn—how to let go of false ideas that act as a wall effectively cutting you off from the awareness of who you really are within the context of a spiritual reality. This unlearning is what Bradshaw means by completing ego work, and is nothing less than your spiritual passport to higher ground. Perhaps, rather than unlearning, *relearning* would be a better description.

And just what is this ego work? We refer to it as *healing any and all unresolved issues residing in consciousness.* And how do you recognize an unresolved issue when you meet one? Easy!

> *Principle #8: An unresolved issue is anything that disturbs your peace.*

The eighth principle of *Seeing Through Soul-Centered Eyes* is extremely important and bears repeating: *An unresolved issue is anything that disturbs your peace.* And yes, we really do mean *anything,* with no exceptions. "Do you mean all the selfish things my brother did and continues to do that make me angry?" you might be asking. Yes, including those! "How about all the violence going on in the world?" That, too! No exceptions means no exceptions!

Please don't get us wrong. We are not condoning abuse or violence in any form. We're simply saying that there's *what's happening in physical reality,* and then there's *your reaction* to it. These are two separate contexts that we'll explore in great detail in the following chapter. All we're suggesting here is that when your peace has been disturbed, you have an amazing opportunity to make spiritual progress regardless of what you perceive *caused* your upset.

As Bradshaw says, "if you don't do your ego work . . . it will pull you back." Why? Because that work is a vital part of your spiritual curriculum; it's what we're all here for. No matter how high you go into spirit, it is your accumulation of yet-to-be-resolved issues—also known in some cultures as *karma*—that will continually provide you with experiences that present what's unresolved. The dynamic is like a rubber band. It can be stretched just so far before it snaps back (or breaks).

Spiritual evolvement, then, is largely a process of letting go and relearning. In order to grasp the nature of such a process, it's helpful to know a little about the structure of consciousness and how it functions. Such an understanding provides tremendous leverage in assisting you in your evolutionary progression.

So let's grab the lamp of exploration and see what you can discover that will assist you on your journey of awakening.

The Ego

In a way, the ego has received way too much bad press, especially among the throngs of spiritual seekers. I remember going to an evening meditation back in my early college days when spirituality was the latest craze and everyone was an aspiring yogi. In preparation, one young man was busy fluffing up his meditation pillow and telling a friend, "I think I've got it figured out. All I have to do is kill my ego." I sincerely hope he didn't succeed, since if he did, I suspect he surely would have perished from the earth at the time.

Humans don't have egos so that they should kill them. In fact, most people need them as long as they're going to participate on the stage of life played out in physical-world reality. Egos are really good at producing results in service to fulfilling desires and ambitions that exist on the Goal Line. Further, it's important to understand that it's largely through the ego that you do any work in this world, spiritual or otherwise.

The challenge of the ego is not that it's bad, but rather that it's old—in a primitive sense. Egos are mechanisms designed to support survival, safety, and security. If a hungry saber-toothed tiger was eyeing you, it was necessary to instantly recognize the danger and mobilize your energy to get out of the way fast. And today, since the vast majority of the world's population is concerned with survival, safety, and security, it isn't surprising that egos continue to dominate the global stage.

Egos, however, aren't designed to support the evolution of consciousness past a certain point, which corresponds to the movement from the perspective of physical-world reality to the context of spiritual reality. They can't perceive the higher frequencies of spirit and weren't designed to function there (and you'll see why soon). While humans as a species are transitioning to higher levels of consciousness, it's important to learn how to utilize your ego in support of your spiritual goals while engaging in the process of awakening.

The ego—which is another way of saying the personality, or small self—is composed of awareness on two distinct levels of consciousness: the mind and the emotions. Both levels are closely related and work in alignment with each other, but both are very limited in what they can observe. Because egos can only function within the mind and emotions, they're only able to know *about* the Soul or Spirit as a concept or a feeling.

Paradoxically, *it's by learning to work effectively within the ego levels that you complete your spiritual curriculum, and in so doing, automatically transcend the ego.* Said another way, it's precisely within the ego levels that you need to shine your lamp of exploration, since most unresolved issues are to be found within the ego's structure. Why? Because unresolved issues comprise ideas (mind) and emotions (energy the mind uses to take action in the world).

Flattering or not, the truth is that most of us have been conditioned to an egotistical approach to life. We've been taught that being successful in the world is what life is all about—Goal Line living. So, in order to maintain its integrity, the ego uses a wide variety of methods to support this philosophy. It sees itself at the center of the universe around which everything and everyone else revolves. It conceives of itself as a separate entity and often spends a great deal of time and effort in search of another ego that reminds it of itself. If and when it finds such a match, it calls the nature of the relationship "love" and goes to great lengths to keep that person nearby and under its control.

Egos live a lonely existence. We were just talking about this earlier today, and Mary remarked that it would be surprising if there wasn't a high correlation between narcissism and loneliness.

⚬∽⚬∽

The ego's drama begins to get interesting when you enter the conscious process of spiritual awakening, which is done by everyone sooner or later. In this process, you open experientially to an essential part of yourself that exists outside of the ego's reality. Prior to that, the ego didn't have so much as an inkling that higher consciousness existed, except as an interesting idea you may have read or heard about. In other words, there comes a time when the ego becomes aware of what is taking place outside the mind or emotions. When this spiritual opening or awakening begins, the ego isn't particularly thrilled; and usually responds with fear, defensiveness, and resistance. This is certainly understandable and even to be expected; after all, to the ego, a person's experience of opening to non-egoic levels of existence threatens its addiction to control . . . and its very existence.

Spiritual awakening transcends the ego's role precisely because it occurs beyond the bounds of the physical, mental, and emotional dimensions. It happens in the context of spiritual reality. To the ego, the threat of extinction is real. In reaction, it will often attempt to block continued efforts at spiritual development. Some of the methods it will use include doubt, denial, and discounting of the awakening experience itself—thus maintaining the status quo of its current comfort zone. These defense mechanisms and others that are well known in clinical psychology are seen by the ego as both necessary and healthy, since it can't comprehend survival outside the realms of the mind and emotions.

Spiritual awakening is not an easy process for the limited ego to undergo, as the most predominant shift is precisely the loosening of the ego's grip on its definition of itself as the true and only source of who you are. You've probably read accounts of spiritual teachers employing unusual methods to assist their students in the processes of "loosening." Some of these were mentioned in the stories about Dr. Hunter, such as altering habits of eating and sleeping.

Although the ego isn't aware of the Soul until spiritual awakening begins, the Soul is always aware of the ego and its function. As we've mentioned before, the Soul knows its own spiritual curriculum and works through the ego to fulfill it. And while the Soul knows what it's here to do, the ego doesn't appear to have a clue. What the ego does have, however, is direct access to the stage upon which the curriculum of life is enacted. It has this privilege because the play takes place on the physical, mental, and emotional levels. Further, the mental and emotional levels are where unresolved issues reside, and those on a spiritual path do well to learn how to recognize and resolve them.

From our perspective, issue-resolution work is as important to all of us collectively as it is to the individual. Why? Consider the next principle:

Principle #9: *Every time a single person resolves a single issue, angels rejoice and all of humanity moves forward in its evolution.*

This is what we mean by ego work, which we refer to as *working our process.*

The more you heal or clear your unresolved issues, the more you open the channel to enhanced spiritual awareness and, ultimately, the more you contribute to the upliftment of the planet. A good metaphor for the process is like peeling an onion, with the exception that with unresolved issues, it's somewhat more difficult to know when the last layer has been removed.

✑✑

It's precisely this work, this learning how to settle unresolved issues, that forms the basis for a truly Spiritual Psychology. By its very nature, Spiritual Psychology must be much more than an academic study of concepts. It has to be a living, breathing, process-oriented psychology that fosters movement in support of the Soul's evolution. To be effective, it must lead you through successive experiences of awakening. Further, it must provide both a context and practical tools that can foster continued awakening so you are less inclined to fall back asleep.

Functionally, in a spiritual context, learning to work effectively within the structure of the ego is essential. It's within the ego that you can gain access to the issues and patterns in need of healing. Rather than trying to kill your ego, you'll be further ahead by educating it in service to your spiritual curriculum.

So let's shine the lamp of exploration into the ego itself, for that's where you'll find the keys for learning how to accelerate your progress in fulfilling your spiritual curriculum.

The Mental Realm

As beings possessing the power of self-reflection, let's stop the action of the play for a moment and retreat to the inner world of what we refer to as the *Neutral Observer,* the one observing the play with no attachment to, or concern about, outcome. Whether the play is a comedy or a tragedy is of no consequence to the Neutral Observer. It simply *observes*.

What most of you would notice, if you viewed the workings of your mind, is that you appear adrift in a sea of conflicting thoughts, beliefs, attitudes, and values. Your mind is awash in a vast array of swirling material on every conceivable subject. But don't observe what the mind is experiencing, but rather how it's *functioning*.

The mind plays an extremely vital part in the passion play of conscious life. It stores information, defines the way things are based upon prior conditioning, and reasons using the definitions of reality it has developed. One of the best characterizations of the mind we've ever heard was uttered at an early USM graduation. The commencement speaker was Marilyn Ferguson, the author of the classic work *The Aquarian Conspiracy*. She began her talk by welcoming everyone and then said that she herself was a graduate of MSU. While we silently ran through a list of possible institutions, such as Michigan State University, Marilyn went on, "That stands for Making Stuff Up."

The mind is largely involved in the process of figuring things out pertaining to physical-world reality. This process is often called *thinking,* although *sorting* or *rearranging* would be a more accurate description. The mind loves to debate ideas, enter into comparisons, and develop dilemmas. People who have access to a great deal of stored information are said to be very knowledgeable.

Further, the mind tolerates mystery only when there's a possibility of figuring out the mystery. It can't abide a contradiction. Its basis for defining reality is the five senses through which it experiences the physical world within which it operates. Its basic job is survival, and it does this by carefully monitoring the environment. It then directs us toward what it purports to be relatively safe choices and what it has defined as positive outcomes, even when certain propensities are clearly seen by others as destructive.

At the mental level, existence consists of a world of competing alternatives. These are usually defined in black-and-white terms, and people often find themselves going back and forth between one choice and another in an attempt to escape the horns of a dilemma. *Should I stay at my job or get another one? Is it better to work on my current relationship or find someone else? Should I move to another city or stay where I am?* The common aspect of all this activity is choosing between different—and often competing—perspectives, always hoping that our decisions result in enhanced levels of happiness.

Yet at a deeper level, thinking revolves around core beliefs that are held about the nature of reality itself. It's impossible for the mind to think outside the box it has created around these core beliefs. Examples include beliefs about the world, God, and the nature and value of oneself and others. We refer to such core beliefs as *definitions of reality.*

✍∽✍∽

Everything a person experiences is stored and categorized in, and by, the mind. The mind is an amazing computer with an unbelievable amount of memory, although given recent bouts of forgetfulness, we're beginning to suspect that some of the memory chips wear with age! If an experience is well outside the comfort zone of an individual's past learning, or is perhaps extremely painful, the mind may remove it from awareness so as not to have to deal with it at all. This process, which involves defense mechanisms such as repression or suppression, is often found with people who have had early traumatic experiences—for example, a severe accident, assault, or child abuse.

In the delightful movie *Dr. Dolittle,* a physician played by Eddie Murphy discovered he could talk with animals. It was disconcerting to him, to say the least, but nothing he thought an MRI couldn't diagnose. To his dismay, the MRI revealed no explanation. It turns out that the doctor had a gift for conversing with animals from the time he was a little kid. The trouble was that his dad didn't see his ability as a precious gift, but as a fast track into an asylum. He kept telling his son that he was making it up and to forget it. Eventually the boy did, although he obviously didn't really forget it quite well enough. Repression is like that. Sometimes when you least expect it, things just pop up as if they have a mind of their own, and perhaps they do.

For the purposes of this book, it is only necessary to know that the mind is like a huge, exceedingly fast computer that will play any program that's fed into it. The type of programming it has received is largely determined by early conditioning. In other words, your upbringing works in such a way that you will tend to gravitate toward certain experiences and selectively remember particular things a certain way.

Several years ago, Mary and I were hosting a small dinner party with my folks and a few of our friends. Since I'm an only child, one of my mother's delights was to tell stories about my youth. That night I came away from dinner convinced I had a twin brother somewhere who shares my name but who had a much different childhood from the one I recall. That's how different her memory of events was from mine. (Maybe someday I'll even meet my "twin" . . .)

Selective memory isn't bad. It's just a process whereby the ego will tend to recall and interpret experiences so they fit into its definitions of reality. Psychiatrist and author David Hawkins wrote: "Perception is edited observation." A great example of this dynamic in action occurs when USM students work with unresolved issues having to do with their parents. There was one young man who was working with the belief that his parents didn't love him, for which he had a multitude of supporting memories. In an effort to gain insight into his process, he decided to interview his parents about his childhood. During the interview, one of the memories he referenced was the *fact* that they never attended his Little League baseball games.

"But dear," his mom said with great surprise, "we went to all of them. Don't you remember?" Turning to her husband, she continued, "Bob, would you please get the photo album with the pictures of us at the Little League games." Sure enough, there were dozens of pictures—proof positive that the student's memory was in error. This was a major turning point for him in his relationship with his parents, because his mind had to let go of the beliefs it held based on the misinterpretations it had made. He was smart enough to realize that if these memories were inaccurate and predicated on misinterpretations made through distorted perceptual filters, in all probability there were other memories he had filed that were also in need of updating. We've noticed that some people, upon hearing this information, become discouraged. But this is actually good news once they realize that their memories actually support their spiritual curriculum.

Your mind will selectively remember in accordance with your spiritual curriculum, and for this reason the mental level is one of the primary arenas within which you can effectively facilitate exploration and transformation. Like the young man in the preceding example, the nature of the work consists of updating early egocentric programming—which, as we've said, turns out to be more of a reprogramming or reconditioning process.

Since everyone's true nature is Loving, each time you release any ego-based programming, the space revealed is already filled with Love. It's like the sun: even before clouds drift away during the day, sunshine is already present.

We'll have a great deal more to say about the releasing process in a bit. Right now, a little additional information will be useful to establish the context within which you'll be engaging in later chapters.

The Emotional Realm

If the mind is likened to a giant computer and its content to a vast network of files, the mind, like any other machine, requires energy to operate. This is the job of the emotions. Emotions can be thought of as *energy in motion,* and they arise as feeling responses to events in physical-world reality.

But what exactly *is* an emotion? Well, it's a physiological response to a thought or belief. This response then gets anchored in the body as an energetic charge. The intensity of the emotional charge—whether positive or negative—is determined by the degree of importance that the mind has assigned to that particular piece of information. For example, most people would feel more emotionally upset if they lost a wedding ring than if they lost another piece of jewelry that cost the same. That's because they hold a belief that the ring is more significant than the other jewelry. Since the mind processes immense amounts of material, it tends to lump what it considers to be similar things into categories, in the same way a group of similar files might be housed in a single folder for ease of processing. As incredible as it may seem, the mind stores every experience we've ever had in its memory.

The groundbreaking work of neurosurgeon and scientist Dr. Wilder Penfield attests to this amazing phenomenon. In his work with patients suffering from frequent convulsive seizures, Penfield spent some 50 years mapping out the functions of every part of the human brain as a means to better diagnose and treat the devastating effects of his patients' grand mal seizures.

The way he worked at this may seem a bit unusual, but it produced amazing results. Under anesthesia, he would first remove a portion of a patient's skull in order to access the brain. Then the patient was partially awakened, and since the brain has no pain receptors, Penfield would probe different areas in order to locate the affected part, which, once accurately defined, would be surgically removed. It was during the probing process that Penfield discovered a remarkable phenomenon. He would probe in a particular place and the patient would report a pleasant memory—say, when she was three years old at a birthday party. Probed in another brain region, the subject might recall an awful experience she had when she was two involving the time her daddy took her for a stroll in a carriage and it tipped over due to a sudden gust of strong wind. In other words, the patients were both awake and aware of themselves on the operating table and, at the same time, reliving a particular memory.

It's interesting to note that since Penfield did many of these procedures over a span of 50 years, he had the unique opportunity of thoroughly investigating every portion of the human brain. In his epic work *Mystery of the Mind,* he reported that there were only two aspects of consciousness he could never physically locate in the brain: (1) volition or will, and (2) the seat of consciousness itself. He concluded that the core of consciousness doesn't appear to be located in the brain or, for that matter, anywhere in the physical body. As such, consciousness appears to be more a spiritual than a physical phenomenon. We believe it was Larry Dossey, M.D., who introduced the term *nonlocal mind* to describe consciousness as a field within which we all exist.

That is why the emotional level is so important in doing ego work. First, you can use emotional disturbance to alert you when you've gone out of balance. In Spiritual Psychology, we refer to this phenomenon as "school in session," since the way people usually become aware of encountering some element of their Earth-school curriculum is through their emotions. They *feel* upset or distracted. This is the essential awareness that *an unresolved issue is anything that disturbs your peace.* It is this recognition that provides you with a choice: You can allow yourself to be agitated and justifiably rant and rave about what it is that has supposedly flustered you—which, ironically, only serves to strengthen the pattern. Or you can seek to determine what it is about the upsetting circumstance that has disturbed your peace and work to heal it.

In this way, you can use the unsettling experience to identify exactly which of your cherished beliefs has in some way been violated. The more important you've decided a particular belief is to you, the more emotionally disturbed you'll feel when you perceive that it has been breached.

What is it that determines the importance of one belief over another? The answer is simple. The relative importance of any belief was learned from parents or prevailing culture, and assumed to be true. It happens in the early programming. And for those of us more metaphysically oriented, it's believed that we are born with a predisposition to interpret early experience in a particular way concordant with what's called karma in the Eastern traditions. These predispositions, and subsequent misinterpretations, are seeded in consciousness and become the conditioned patterns that define a person's spiritual curriculum.

And once the cultural programming has been accepted, it will run unabated throughout someone's life until the day he or she dies (and perhaps even after) or begins to wake up to the personal power to liberate him- or herself from these limiting constructs. It is for this reason that spiritual development is an individual, and not a group, process. Paraphrasing Ralph Waldo Emerson, one of our favorite teachers, "Souls are not saved in bunches, like bananas."

A Pragmatic Model

One of the challenges regarding waking up is that until you do, no matter how lofty your thoughts about Spirit or God or Universal Truth are, they're just mental concepts. It's only after you've had an awakening experience that you have something beyond concepts to share. But then you're *sharing an experience* rather than attempting to *explain through words and ideas.* According to Polish American scientist, educator, and semanticist Alfred Korzybski, "The map is not the territory."

And while it's true that maps are not territories, they can be very useful as navigational guides until you've learned the territory through direct experience. So if we visualize what we've talked about so far, it looks like this:

Figure 3

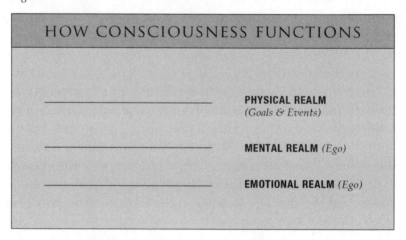

The *physical* realm is the stage upon which life's action is played out. It's everything happening *out there.* It's the level of relationships, career, finances, physical health, family, and so on. These areas are where you look in order to measure success on the Goal Line.

The *mental* realm is part of the ego, personality, or small self. It includes thoughts, beliefs, values, attitudes, and even perceptions of the nature of reality itself that you've either learned while growing up or simply brought forward from previous experience.

Also part of the ego, the *emotional* realm gives power to the thoughts of the mind and provides energy consistent with the ego's estimation of the importance of whatever it's considering. If the ego is concerned with something it deems of little importance, it will provide relatively little energy (mild emotions) to the process. If it's thinking about something it considers very important, it will provide a great deal of energy (intense emotions) to whatever is being considered. This explains why more wars have been fought over religion than anything else. For many people, religion is of major importance. And because it's so important, people often have very strong beliefs and intense emotions when the topic comes up, resulting in extremely righteous positions.

If you look at these three realms a bit more closely, you'll see that what they have in common is the function of polarity, or duality. This is indicated by the vertical line drawn down the middle of the map.

Figure 4

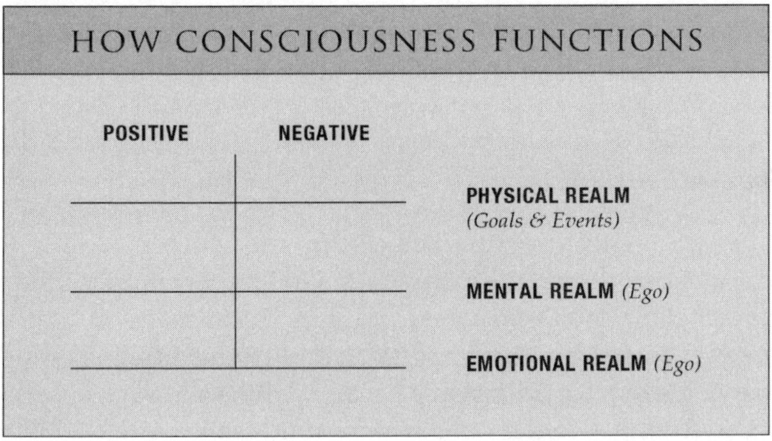

HOW CONSCIOUSNESS FUNCTIONS

POSITIVE   **NEGATIVE**

PHYSICAL REALM
(Goals & Events)

MENTAL REALM *(Ego)*

EMOTIONAL REALM *(Ego)*

The ego conveniently divides all experiences into positive or negative, depending upon how they're defined in the mind. The vertical line is what's called *psychological homeostasis,* or balance point. It's like the middle of a seesaw, with positive experiences on one side and negative experiences on the other. This balance point gives stability to your psychological system. Your feelings will naturally align with the beliefs and definitions of reality that you have about whatever you're considering.

So if you have a job you've defined as "bad," you will tend to have negative feelings when you get up to go to work, especially on Monday morning. Conversely, if you think you have a "great" job, you'll tend to feel good about going to work each morning. The amount of energy allocated to each emotion is determined by your fundamental beliefs about how important things are. Either way, your positive or negative feelings about your job will probably be more powerful than how you feel about the coffee mug sitting on your table, since these two things are ranked by your mind as such.

What's been considered so far is consistent with the domain of most psychological systems. We'll now take our departure into Spiritual Psychology by moving from the dualistic conceptions of the ego into a deeper level of consciousness that operates within a completely different context. It is upon entering this context that the door is opened to what we refer to as the Authentic Self.

The Authentic Self

Beneath/encompassing/behind the ego (do you see the difficulty of describing this reality in mental-level concepts?) resides another dimension of awareness. It's in this dimension that the core of who you are as a spiritual being having a human experience is discovered. To become aware of this level, it is necessary to step from the context of physical-world reality into the higher frequency of spiritual reality. The Authentic Self isn't interested in, nor does it have any concern about, success in the world. It seems to have but one purpose: to gain in wisdom and to grow in its expression of its nature. As we've said, that nature is Love. The

Authentic Self doesn't think or feel. Rather, it exists in a state of perpetual Unconditional Love.

Figure 5

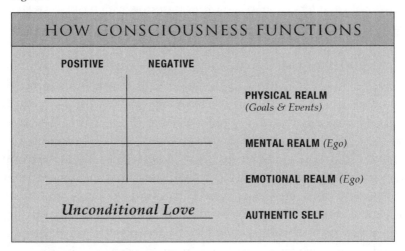

People who meditate are working to strengthen their conscious connection with the Authentic Self. This part of consciousness is the gateway to the spiritual dimensions that have been written about and described since ancient times.

Your Authentic Self knows the curriculum you've come here to learn. It knows what ego work you're here to complete. It also knows that until your ego work is done, your spiritual agenda in the physical world will serve you by continually providing experiences that will tend to trigger your unresolved issues. These experiences, when viewed from within the context of the Authentic Self, are actually spiritual opportunities to learn, grow, and complete what must be done. Although, truth be told, they can and often do appear to be extremely challenging from both a physical and a psychological perspective. The Authentic Self cooperates with this structure, for it knows what it's here to do and how this physical form supports its spiritual progression.

One of the first things you'll notice about the Authentic Self level is that there is no duality. When you find yourself at this level, all you will ever experience is Unconditional Love, Compassion, Peace, Acceptance, Infinite Patience, Gratitude, Wisdom, and Joy. Many people assume that these qualities are emotional states or feelings. But they're not, because they don't reside in the duality of the emotional level. These qualities describe a state of being that's continual and has no opposite.

When you find yourself infused with any of these qualities, it's an indicator that you've shifted into a higher frame of reference within which everything that's happening to you is still happening, only now it's all seen as a blessing. *Nothing has changed outwardly, yet you are at Peace or, more accurately, in Peace.* When this occurs, you are literally observing from within a different context in consciousness, and it's only from this place that you can actually see what's *real*. In contrast, when you look from the ego levels of the mind and emotions, you see through the perceptual filters of your conditioned beliefs and limiting interpretations of reality. This results in distortions; generalizations; and even the deleting of certain, and one would think pertinent, data so as to more closely match your beliefs. As someone once said, "Please don't confuse me with the facts."

When you are seeing from the level of the Authentic Self, you are seeing from a more expansive context devoid of dualistic perception. As William Blake wrote in his illustrated poetic work *The Marriage of Heaven and Hell,* "If the doors of perception were cleansed every thing would appear to man as it is: infinite." You can only *see* clearly when you are *seeing* through the eyes of the Authentic Self. This is what we mean by *Seeing Through Soul-Centered Eyes.*

And herein lies one of the keys to the value and power of Spiritual Psychology. Working within conventional psychological systems, the goal is usually to foster more constructive behavior, more rational thought processes, greater emotional maturity, or some combination of these. The aim is always a more fulfilling life largely measured on the Goal Line—and this is, of course, valuable work.

In Spiritual Psychology, however, the primary aim is to complete your spiritual curriculum. The way to do this is to learn to work with unresolved psychological "material" by drawing it into the level of the Authentic Self, where it dissolves. Ironically, the automatic by-product of completing spiritual curriculum by resolving unresolved issues is that the quality of your life invariably improves. Let's see what this process might look like. . . .

Consciousness in Motion

Suppose you sincerely decided that weight release is an aim you wish to pursue on the Goal Line in physical-world reality. You've set that as a clear intention and lined up a health-care practitioner to support you. Furthermore, by coincidence, you've recently met a wonderful weight-release specialist who has chosen you as a role model to demonstrate her good work. Under her tutelage, you're diligent about your process and—lo and behold—you've released 25 pounds within three months. What you've accomplished in physical-world reality is to transform what used to be negative energy, thus expanding the positive energy, as you can see in Figure 6.

Figure 6

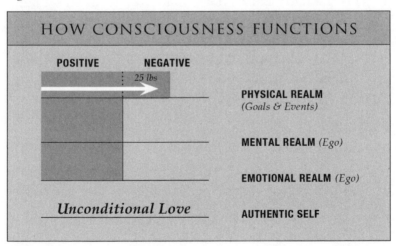

You may wonder, *Why is the arrow moving into the negative?* Shouldn't it be moving into the positive to show the positive direction of what you've accomplished? Good question. The arrow moves into the negative to signify that you've successfully *transformed* a certain amount of what used to be negative energy into positive energy. In fact, we can even measure it. It's 25 pounds' worth of energy. So far, so good.

But look! You've also disturbed the homeostatic balance in your psychological system. The mental and emotional levels are no longer in alignment with the physical level. Experientially, you're probably feeling somewhat vulnerable and perhaps more easily agitated. Not to worry! Whenever you experiment with new behavior, it pushes on your comfort zone. All learning begins with venturing into new territory that was previously unknown. Otherwise, it wouldn't be learning.

So here you are, somewhat out of balance internally. A message goes out into your consciousness saying something like: "You are demonstrating that you want a change in consciousness by taking action in physical-world reality, which is producing the desired result of weight release. It appears you want to establish a more positive balance point to support the 25-pound weight release. You intend to experience the consciousness that goes along with a thinner you and to establish homeostatic balance at a more positive level than you had previously." In our diagram, the line of dashes is what this intention would look like.

Figure 7

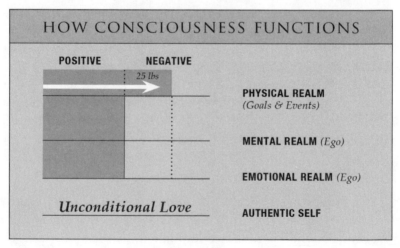

78

Again, so far, so good. It is at this juncture that the game gets interesting. What will happen next is that all of the *mental* and related *emotional* material that was associated with why you gained the 25 pounds in the first place is going to come bubbling up to the surface for you to heal. These are represented by the X's in Figure 8. This surfacing action is actually a consequence of the changes you've already made by releasing the 25 pounds. You've earned the right to see and work with whatever the weight was protecting.

Figure 8

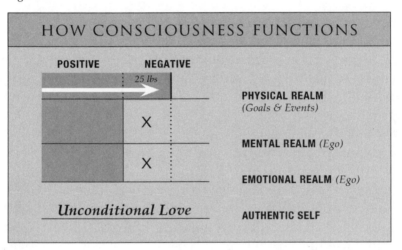

Whenever I think about this process, I'm reminded of a wonderful quote by Jimmy Breslin I recall reading in *The New York Times* many years ago. It went something like: "When you stop drinking, you have to deal with this marvelous personality that started you drinking in the first place." He was so right, and while it might be uncomfortable in the short term, the process of dealing with that "marvelous personality" (ego) is necessary in order to get to where you want to go—establishing psychological balance at an enhanced level of functioning. Within the context of Spiritual Psychology, we would say that your Soul is using this experience for purposes of awakening by providing you with the opportunity to resolve an issue or pattern anchored in the ego levels of consciousness, which was previously reflected physically by your weight.

You might wonder what happens if you don't do the healing ego work regarding what's surfacing. Well, since many weight-release programs don't address healing at the mental and emotional levels, it's not surprising how research studies indicate that approximately 95 percent of all people who release significant weight gain it back within five years. Why? Because the post-diet, thinner person hasn't been taught how to resolve the mental and emotional issues at the ego levels, and this is necessary to support and sustain the shift in consciousness that was initiated by releasing the weight. So if people don't do the inner work, all that will happen is that they'll gravitate back toward where they started because they can't tolerate the homeostatic imbalance for long. It's too uncomfortable.

And what might the mental/emotional work be? Using the preceding example, weight release may bring to the surface issues of intimacy because extra weight is often added as a means of protection. On the emotional level, the individual may tend to fear hurt associated with past experiences of perceived rejection or disapproval, or perhaps feels shame or holds a hidden hunger for love. On the mental level, this person's concept of self may be impoverished, which would result in deep feelings of unworthiness expressed at the emotional level.

Assuming the inner healing work is successful, this person will be able to maintain the new weight, which is reflected in this chapter's final diagram.

Figure 9

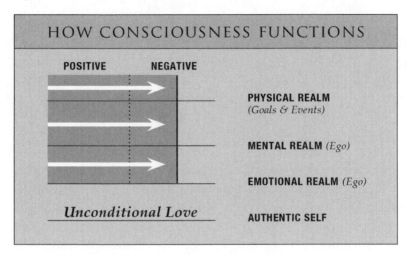

Can you see the incredible opportunity your spiritual curriculum provides for you every day of your life? No matter what you do, your spiritual agenda will ensure that you look out at life through eyes that see according to where you are in your evolutionary development *whether you are conscious of it or not.*

Maggie's Story

Maggie, a USM graduate, is an excellent example of this process. She was overweight to the point of obesity and had been most of her life. As part of her personal-growth work, she decided to address this situation once and for all. She proceeded to set herself up for success by choosing a weight-release specialist who assisted her in establishing a sound nutritional program. Part of the specialist's program included weekly visits so that he could continually support and encourage her to stick with the prescribed diet and exercise routine, as well as monitor her overall health and well-being.

As the months went by, Maggie released weight at exactly the rate the specialist was hoping she would—not too much and not too little at a time. Because Maggie was a friend, we periodically asked how she was doing mentally and emotionally on the eating program. We suspected that a great deal of material was probably surfacing, and we were aware she might require support in doing the work necessary to sustain the release. She'd always say that she was focusing exclusively on a behavioral approach to releasing the excess weight. To her, the *learning* was all about the discipline necessary to shed the pounds. She was engaged in her process in a rather rigid, militaristic manner, focused exclusively on the Goal Line.

Slowly and noticeably, Maggie's appearance was transforming. Indeed, day by day before our eyes, her outer beauty was aligning more and more with her inner beauty. When she reached her goal, she turned out to be a petite woman whose beautiful smile, which she always wore, now seemed even more radiant relative to her much smaller body. All in all, she had released some 160 pounds, and she was gorgeous. So it was not surprising that Maggie began attracting the attention of men who were interested in her.

Suddenly, she'd run smack into a major issue having to do with protection from, and fear of, intimacy. It was this unresolved topic that had resulted in her putting on the excess weight in the first place. And since she hadn't been doing very much mental and emotional clearing throughout her releasing process, she was unprepared for the thoughts and feelings surfacing in her consciousness.

The vulnerability of her small body was no match for the huge insecurity that had been triggered. It was too much for her to handle, and as we might anticipate, the weight began to re appear. Ultimately, she gained it all back. We're glad to report that, as of this writing, she's again involved in the process of releasing weight. Only this time she is going about it in a more gentle, yet disciplined, manner while also compassionately addressing the mental and emotional material as it surfaces. We're confident she will be more successful this time.

❧❧

When you begin catching on to the nature and dynamics of the process, you see that ego work is a vital part of a Soul's curriculum. This is a radical departure from most psychological systems. The art and science of Spiritual Psychology is about learning how to use life's precious energy in service to your Souls' curriculum, how to use everyday experiences as rungs on the ladder of your spiritual evolution. Your highest goal is to take full advantage of this earthly existence as a spiritual opportunity and, like the prodigal son or daughter, to find your way back Home again.

As we've mentioned, the heart of this journey is what we call *working your process,* and it's the cornerstone of Spiritual Psychology. Many students have heard me say in class over the years: Every time anyone is successful at working their process and heals an unresolved issue, they have freed themselves from one of the bonds that ties them to the suffering of the *Earth School.*

Stem Sentences to Write Down and Contemplate

- If some of my memories are inaccurate, then . . .
- If my feelings stem from my thoughts, then . . .
- What disturbs my peace is . . .

Repeat as often as necessary.

CHAPTER FIVE

I Am Upset Because . . .

Angry people are like storms: at their core, they're peaceful.
When times appear stormy, always move toward your
Center, for it's there where you'll find your peace.

Several years prior to my experiences with Dr. Hunter in New Mexico, I was driving around the streets of Brooklyn, New York, selling floor waxes, of all things. It wasn't the most exciting work for a young man eager to find his place in the world, but nevertheless that's what I was doing . . . perhaps a form of laying the groundwork for what was to come.

One day while I was on my way to my next appointment, my radio was tuned to WBAI, a listener-sponsored station in New York, and I heard an amazing program. It was a lecture called "The Transformation of a Man" given by former Harvard professor Richard Alpert, who had become a spiritual seeker now going by the name Ram Dass.

He talked about his recent trip to India, where he had met his spiritual teacher, and it was the first time I had ever heard anything quite like it. Or had I?

Let me pause here, for as I recall this incident in my life, I'm reminded of Dr. Hunter's words to me in Alamogordo: "You've had this awareness many times before. You just didn't recognize it for what it was because you had no conceptual reference by which to evaluate it. You've known about the reality of Spirit from the time you were born. That's why you've always questioned the meaning of life and why you majored in psychology."

I was so intrigued by what I was hearing that I completely forgot my appointment and pulled over and listened to that radio show for more than three hours. One of the things Ram Dass quoted his teacher as saying fascinated me: "No matter what is happening in your life, you can experience contentment." What a concept! The impact of that idea was immediate and stunning.

I remember thinking: *I can do this. No one has ever presented this possibility to me before, and I've never thought of it myself. But why should life's events make me feel a certain way? From this moment on, I'm going to choose to experience contentment no matter what's happening.*

Interestingly, I was actually able to choose contentment regardless of circumstance for about two weeks. Alas, my consciously chosen contentment didn't last long. I had no idea at the time that I couldn't decide to be more conscious in the same way I could chose a turkey sandwich over chicken. It's not quite that simple. For the next two weeks, despite my best intentions, life continued to present me with situations designed to surface unresolved disturbances residing within my ego-centered consciousness—which, of course, had remained intact. In the end, I could no longer hold the level of consciousness needed to sustain the "contentment no matter what" approach. It was just as John Bradshaw said, "If you don't do your ego work . . . it will pull you back."

It's not that the sense of contentment fell away one day; it's more as if it eroded over time. Because the choice wasn't based upon true issue resolution, my ego-based, perceptual reality eventually reasserted itself. But for those initial two weeks, I was higher than a kite. No matter what anyone said or did, an inner smile emerged, and I consciously chose contentment.

I didn't realize it at the time, but my two-week experiment in choosing my response proved something significant: *Events don't have to automatically make me feel a certain way.* Ram Dass's teacher was right! Things I didn't like had no real power to make me experience negative feelings. And, if that was so, things I *did* like held no real power to make me feel happy. The assumption that our feelings are *because* of something happening outside us is inaccurate and illusory for both happy and unhappy emotions. (As a side note, I realized then that the only reason psychology focuses on negative feelings is because people don't sign up for therapy when they're so happy they can't stand it.)

This revelation flies in the face of popular belief. For example, suppose someone is involved in a less-than-satisfying relationship. In an ego-based sense of personal wisdom, that person might say, "I don't want to be in this relationship. It's not working for me. And the only chance of it working better is if my partner changes."

If you find yourself reaching this kind of conclusion in response to many of your life's challenges, rest assured that you're not alone. In fact, you've expressed the single most prevalent myth rampant in our culture today: *Everything in my life would be fine if only just a few things were happening differently. It's those things happening the way they are that makes me feel upset.*

And so our disturbance is expressed by saying something similar to: "I am upset because . . ." Here are some common examples you may have heard:

- "I am upset because people don't listen to me."
- "I am upset because people don't understand me."
- "I am upset because my spouse didn't call."
- "I am upset because I don't have a spouse."
- "I am upset because my boss sent me a particular e-mail."
- "I am upset because I don't make enough money."
- "I am upset because politicians have little integrity."
- "I am upset because you don't worship my God."

And on and on it goes. Almost all of us have been conditioned to relate to the world through an "I am upset because . . ." philosophy.

In fact, this approach is epidemic on the planet and carries huge negative consequences. To check this out for yourself, just turn on any news channel or read a major newspaper anywhere in the world on any given day; you will see story after story about someone blaming someone else for his or her disturbance. While it's almost impossible to comprehend, you're probably only too aware that there are those willing to go as far as killing themselves and others they blame as the "because" of their plight.

It has even gotten to the point where the "I am upset because . . ." claim is rewarded in the court system with immense sums of money. We recently read a news report about a woman who successfully sued a clothing store because it failed to prevent a small child from running around the store, and the woman was injured when she tripped over him. Toward the end of the story, the article casually mentioned that it was her own child whom she tripped over. We kid you not. (No pun intended.)

And thus we come to the crux of the matter. "I am upset because . . ." is a complete and total victim position. It's an attitude that places the responsibility for one's emotional condition outside of oneself.

One of our all-time favorite cartoons showed a picture of three shabbily dressed panhandlers who are standing next to each other in front of a building in a large city. Each is holding up a sign. The first guy's sign says, VICTIM OF CHILD ABUSE. The second sign reads: VICTIM OF SOCIETY'S POOR EDUCATIONAL SYSTEM. The third sign says: RESULT OF POOR CHOICES. The first guy has turned to the second guy and remarks about the third: "He's never going to get anything with that approach."

Let's take a closer look at this extremely important dynamic because, in many ways, "I am upset because . . ." is a very tempting route to take in the world, precisely because it seems so very logical and is a popular method that results in our feeling justified and righteous.

The Dynamics of a Disturbance

When you hear someone saying "I am upset because . . ." are you hearing his or her ego or Authentic Self expressing itself?

Since the very expression of pain or disturbance can only occur in the mind and emotions, there can be no doubt that "I am upset because . . ." is an ego experience. And since the ego always wants to be *right,* it must create a dynamic such that it can be *right* even in situations when it knows it's behaving poorly, such as destructive expressions of anger. Thus, "I am upset because . . ." emerges as the perfect solution by which the ego can engage in negative behavior and still be *right.* How clever!

If you say, "I am upset because . . ." and you want to change something so that you would no longer feel upset, where would you seek to intervene? You would no doubt direct your energy into attempting to bring about change at the "because" level. You would logically reason, "If I can change the person or situation upsetting me, I will no longer feel upset." It makes perfectly good sense. And off you go in an effort to change someone or something *out there.*

Have you noticed that such attempts at effecting outer change, in those rare times that you're successful, can produce a temporary reduction in upset but rarely produce the long-term equanimity you're seeking? In the long run, are you ever any happier as a result of experiencing a disruption? Have you ever noticed that when you're upset and expressing yourself in out-of-balance ways, people often ignore and discount your demands? And even if you are successful in getting others to acquiesce to your annoyance, you're often left with the collateral damage to the relationship.

The "I am upset because . . ." dynamic is so ingrained in most people's awareness that when we present it, we often hear, "Do you mean there's an alternative?" Actually, there is!

Contrary to popular opinion, might it be that inner disturbance isn't *caused* by outer experience? Might it just be the other way around? Might it be that *inner, chronic disturbance* is being acted out in repeated outer disturbances? *And further, might this inner disturbance be "Soul-orchestrated" in service to learning a more direct and healthy approach to addressing the inner disturbance itself?*

For example, might it be that someone's disturbance about certain governmental rules, regulations, and laws is actually the surfacing of an unresolved issue with authority? If you don't understand how disturbance actually works in consciousness, you could easily believe that politicians affiliated with _____(enter here whichever political party you disagree with) are ruining the country. It would be easy to blame them because you don't know how to accept responsibility as the *author* of your experiences, and because it's so much easier to blame someone else for your upset. Without a working knowledge of how to resolve these disturbances in consciousness, it's easy to adopt the above victim-oriented position and experience all the suffering that comes with it. We call this *self-created victimization*.

And, yes, you can certainly take steps to improve social and economic conditions. And, yes, you can work to change laws and the governments that make them. But these outer activities will do little, if anything, to alleviate the inner sense of discouragement and lack of fulfillment. The good news is that there's nothing to stop you from working on both levels simultaneously. One does not preclude the other.

Over the years, we've noticed that when an inner disturbance is resolved, someone's effectiveness in making a positive difference in the world actually improves. In fact, changes often occur around such a person that appear to have nothing to do with anything he or she has done outwardly. Some refer to this occurrence as co-incidence. We call it *Grace*.

They Were Very Messy People

Susan was a USM student whose in-laws were staying with her for an extended period of time. (This is not necessarily a good idea—but that's another story.) One Saturday evening, she shared with the class that she was infuriated at her guests because they were very messy people, and she prided herself on keeping her home immaculate. Their sloppiness was driving her crazy. As she put it, "I don't believe they know the meaning of the word *neat*."

Susan wanted to work on her disturbance because she was afraid that if she approached her in-laws from an attitude of resentment, she would probably say things she'd later regret. She was also concerned that she might even embarrass her husband—the last thing she wanted to do. What she did want was to approach her spouse's parents from a balanced and caring place inside of herself.

Right then and there, she did a significant piece of inner work, getting in touch with the part inside of her that judges messiness. In the course of the process, Susan had a deep healing experience in which she recognized how her own obsession with neatness and order reflected her desire for control. When she saw this pattern in her own consciousness, she experienced Compassion and Acceptance first for herself and then for her in-laws. She shared that she felt much clearer and *in balance* with respect to them.

Further, she realized, not as a concept but as a new sense of reality: "Just because I perceive they are messing up my house doesn't mean I have to judge them and make them wrong. I can talk this over with my husband in a caring way and request what I'd like. I'm confident he'd be more than willing for us to pay for them to stay at a hotel if my request doesn't work for them, and I need to check this out with him. But the main thing is, I don't have to approach them antagonistically. I don't have to make them wrong. I can communicate my request in a loving way."

Susan wanted to "strike while the iron was hot," meaning while she was in her newfound clarity. She committed to going home right after class and speaking with her husband in preparation for having an honest heart-to-heart talk with her in-laws about this situation. She promised to report back to us in the morning.

As you might imagine, the next day Susan had her hand up first to share, and as she stood up to talk, we were all ears. "You're not going to believe this! When I got home last night, not only was the house clean, but everything had been put back in its place!"

Although she was ready to confront them compassionately and clearly, there was no need. Somehow they'd received the message and responded accordingly on their own.

There are those who would explain such an event as a lovely and fortunate coincidence. However, we've seen this sort of thing happen so often that the word *coincidence* simply doesn't explain the data very well. Rather, we've observed that once people successfully do a piece of inner work, they are literally living within a new inner reality, and the outer reality will often come into alignment with it. We believe this is what Ralph Waldo Emerson meant in the talk he delivered to the Phi Beta Kappa Society at Harvard University on August 31, 1837. In the ending lines of his well-known and well-received address entitled "The American Scholar," he told the audience, ". . . if the single man plant himself indomitably on his instincts, and there abide, the huge world will come round to him."

Disturbance Is an Inside Job

To see how this approach fits into Spiritual Psychology and why it's so essential, let's consider "I am upset because . . ." in the light of levels of consciousness:

— *I am* is the only true statement that can ever be uttered. It's a declaration from the Soul identifying itself. Anything more will be commentary about what the Soul is experiencing, mostly through the ego's perceptions.

— *Upset* is a description of the state of the ego, small self, or personality. It is experienced as an emotional state and is usually what's meant when someone says, "I am upset." Actually, upon closer examination you'll find that emotional reactions are simply physiological responses to your thoughts based upon your perceptions and beliefs, as previously stated.

— *Because* is the method the ego uses to point at whatever it perceives as causing its disturbance. People tend to think they need a *cause* to blame so that they can justify their inner state of disturbance, as well as any resulting behavior: "What so-and-so did is a good reason for the way I feel and a justification for my actions, which *he* caused by whatever it was he did that I didn't like."

Here's the short course in how it works: You perceive through your perceptual filters, which are determined by what you believe to be true—your definitions of reality. These definitions are usually built upon limiting interpretations of early experience. The interpretations stem directly from your individual spiritual curriculum, which predisposes you to see in a particular way. Thus, something happens, your mind interprets it as good or bad according to its previously determined definitions regarding such experiences, and you react emotionally. Your reaction is one of happiness if you've defined the event as good or of upset if you've defined the event as bad. The intensity of the emotional reaction, positive or negative, will be congruent with the level of importance the ego has attached to whatever has happened.

As we've said, disturbances are always found in the mind and emotions. Later in the book, we'll go into greater detail about how to use this awareness in service to issue resolution. In fact, we'll be presenting you with a comprehensive step-by-step healing process.

An Upset in Search of a Good "Because"

Have you ever noticed that sometimes a particular thing bothers you while other times the very same thing doesn't? Doesn't this give the game away? Doesn't this unmask the false claim of cause and effect paraded in "I am upset because . . ."?

And have you also noticed that, even after you've fussed and fumed and blamed and condemned someone for "upsetting" you, the unrest doesn't go away? That surely reveals inner disturbance to be a chronic, internal state rather than a onetime, outer-caused occurrence.

Agitation also appears to be cumulative in that it builds in consciousness until it reaches a point where it can no longer be contained. At that point you're set to blow up at the slightest provocation. Just prior to your blowup, unbeknownst to you, you've actually been walking around looking for something to become upset about. At such times, you're an "upset in search of a good because."

Those whose inner disturbances are easily triggered and intense are said to be on a "short fuse." We try to avoid such people as much as possible so as not to become a target for their blame. They always have a good reason for their chronic suffering, and they tend to be very righteous about their victim position.

Can you see how the "I am upset because . . ." approach (philosophy) erroneously assigns power to another person? Think about it. If an annoyance is externally caused, where is the power? If "I am upset because you cut me off in traffic" or "I am upset because you left the cap off the toothpaste," then I have disempowered myself. I have effectively given my power over to you, and you can disturb my peace anytime you want by simply engaging in the behavior I've defined as objectionable.

When you think about all the things that have frustrated you lately, you may begin to become aware of how unwittingly you've disempowered and victimized yourself. By engaging in "I am upset because . . ." you're giving your power away to others.

So what can you do? For starters, you can accept the possibility that, whether you know it or not, you're evolving spiritually. Further, if you learn to utilize all of life's experiences for spiritual purposes—perhaps the most important of which is the resolution of issues—anything that disturbs your peace presents you with a golden opportunity. As stated in the third principle of *Seeing Through Soul-Centered Eyes*, physical-world reality exists for the purpose of spiritual evolution.

Attention: You've Just Entered a Reconstruction Zone

One of the hallmarks of Spiritual Psychology is the recognition that what disturbs you is as clear an indicator of your Soul's curriculum as you're likely to ever get—once you learn to see it within that context. When you become upset, it's as if life has just waved a big red flag signaling: "Attention! This is it! Look here! Here's the inner work that's next for you to do. Here's an opportunity to heal the place inside where this disturbance resides. Don't look outside. What happened is simply a triggering device intended to surface the disturbance. Take back your ownership of the disturbance and use it to heal the place inside that's in pain and separation. By so doing, you reclaim your power."

In our work over the years, we've found that as people develop in spiritual awareness, they come to the realization that it's their Souls, the very essence of who or what they truly are, that are bringing forward whatever it is that they need to experience next in service to their growth. Each negative feeling can actually be considered a spiritual opportunity to work with it and possibly heal or resolve it for the very last time.

Of course, like all good things in life, this is easier said than done. Most of us haven't been brought up this way. Rather, we've been trained to live an "I am upset because . . ." life without even being aware that there's another possibility. People actually believe that their *core definitions of reality* are the *real* reality. They avoid awareness of the subjective nature of personal reality. Rather than saying, "I'm currently perceiving myself as a victim," they're more apt to say, "No, I really *am* a victim because such and such happened to me. That's really how it is!" or "Get real! It's just the way things are!"

To be successful in your endeavor of spiritual awakening, you need to change priorities and turn your focus away from an obsession with Goal Line reality as all there is. You must dare to journey into the very structure of your consciousness and carefully examine the dynamics of how the ego functions. However, you need to do your examination within the context of Spiritual Psychology, for you'll never graduate to inner Peace and Love by attempting to intervene solely at the *because* level, since it's the ego's domain. This brings us to the tenth Soul-Centered principle:

> *Principle #10: All "becauses" are merely triggers to internal unresolved issues inviting completion.*

As the Authentic Self would say, "The process of becoming upset doesn't happen outside of myself. It happens within." Well then, what if the same thing happened and you *didn't have to become upset?* Wouldn't it be valuable to know that and learn how to master that dynamic?

What if all *becauses* were seen as methods for bringing your spiritual curriculum into your awareness? In this way of looking, the primary place to focus effort would not be on the *becauses,* but rather on the place in your consciousness where the disturbance itself resides.

After all, isn't it obvious that healing does *not* occur out there? True healing only happens within the consciousness of one single human being at a time. It's an inside job. And might it just be that this is the way humanity evolves? If this way of viewing life is valid, it would follow, as stated in the ninth principle: *Every time a single person resolves a single issue, angels rejoice and all of humanity moves forward in its evolution.*

So if *becauses* are merely triggers to internal processes, what are these processes and why are they operating in our reality? We contemplated this question for a long time until, one day, the following principle dawned on us:

> **Principle #11:** *Inner disturbances are themselves a major component of the spiritual curriculum you are here to complete.*

What a concept! In this context, anger, hurt, resentment, betrayal, abandonment, guilt, shame, rejection, disappointment, sadness, and so on are all spiritual curricula encoded into our consciousness to provide us with the God-given opportunities to heal or complete these unresolved issues for the last time.

This is an astonishing awareness. When you're willing to take responsibility for healing the disturbed places in your own consciousness, you have a way you can grow spiritually that is totally within your dominion and not dependent upon changing anything outside of yourself. At last, you have stumbled upon the empowering key that unlocks the "I am upset because . . ." dilemma. What you need to do is go inside and work directly with the place in consciousness experiencing the upset. Suddenly, by that simple shift in focus, the gateway to freedom appears in the form of the next principle:

> **Principle #12:** *Unresolved issues are not bad; they are just part of your spiritual curriculum and are an opportunity for healing.*

The ego would argue: "Nonsense! I'm justified in feeling the way I do when awful things happen. In fact, those who don't feel angry and outraged at injustices are not only brain-dead, but also cold and aloof and probably in denial."

The Authentic Self would gently and lovingly reply: "It's those very feelings of anger and outrage that you've come to heal. Once you heal them, when things happen that are not to your liking, you are free from emotional upset and can choose to use your energy to address the challenging situation with wisdom, caring, and effectiveness."

Early Learning Is by Association

Freud has yet to be disproved in his assertion that the basic personality structure is laid down in the human infant prior to the age of five. Moreover, developmental psychologists have determined that cognitive reasoning as a mode of functioning comes into prominence at around age six. Isn't that interesting? If these two observations are accurate, it means that basic personality structure is being formulated prior to the child's ability to reason! How do younger children learn—up to age six—if *not* by reason?

The answer seems to be that early learning is by association. As poet Sondra Anice Barnes penned:

> *The siren blew;*
> *The dishwasher*
> *Broke down.*
> *Now I know*
> *That sirens*
> *Break dishwashers*

(From the Brason-Sargar publication: *Life Is The Way It Is,* copyright 1978 and 1980 Sondra Anice Barnes and used with her permission.)

Let's imagine that I'm around 18 months old, playing in my crib with my toys. There's a noise at the door, so I look up. Wow! Here comes Mommy, and she has her arms out for little Ronnie. I know from previous associational experience that this means she's going to pick me up and we're going to cuddle, which is what I love best. So I stand up, put a big smile on my face, and reach out to her as she's bending down for me . . . and then something happens: she turns around and walks away.

Now remember, I'm only 18 months old. I don't know anything about telephones, doorbells, teakettles, or any of the other possible things that could have called her away at that moment. All I know is that she left.

Of course, if I'm an 18-month-old, Self-realized, awakened spiritual master, I would say, "Huh, isn't that interesting? I wonder why she went away? Oh well, she'll be back soon enough, and in the meantime, I'll just have fun and build some piles with my blocks."

But I'm not an 18-month-old, Self-realized, awakened spiritual master. I'm an ordinary Soul learning through human experience. And I'm so devastated that I start to cry. Right then and there, I've begun to learn through association that *loving* and *leaving* go together.

And if *rejection* or *abandonment* is part of the spiritual curriculum I came to work on and possibly complete in this lifetime, that pattern has now been "seeded" in my consciousness. I've now embarked upon a career of being attracted to and falling in love with women who will probably leave me. And if they don't of their own volition, I will most likely unconsciously push them away to validate the belief that people who love me will leave me, because the two are paired in my consciousness.

It's interesting how the psychology community has tended to look at these sorts of mechanisms and sought to explain them in terms of an almost Newtonian, cause-and-effect dynamic. Traditional psychology tells us that Ronnie's rejection pattern was "caused" by his early relationship with his mother, who rejected him.

But is this really an explanation, much less *the* explanation? Or is it a description of an illusion? If it were truly a cause-and-effect dynamic, then wouldn't all men who were seemingly rejected by their mothers have a lifelong rejection pattern? But they don't. Even siblings growing up in the same family have radically different interpretations of the same event. Isn't that a clue to the subjective nature of personal reality?

I recall one of my earliest experiences in a group-therapy

encounter of the type popular in the '60s. Everyone was taking turns going around a circle engaging in what today would be called some serious parent bashing. For example, "I'm the way I am because my parents didn't love me enough and did this to me and that to me."

When it got around to the last guy, he said, "Wow, I'm really amazed by everything I've heard. My parents treated me in all the ways you've all shared that your parents treated you, but somehow I always knew that that was their stuff and had nothing to do with me. So I never took any of it personally." Amazing! How did he know that?

If we stick with a purely psychological, cause-and-effect explanation for human sadness and pain, we'll be going around in philosophical circles for a long time because there is really no way to prove or disprove any such theory. However, once we shift into a context of Spiritual Psychology, we open the field for discovery. We begin to see that each and every Soul is born into the Earth School, as Dr. Hunter liked to call it, with a specific curriculum. And that curriculum predisposes our developing egos to make certain interpretations of early experiences so that the patterns we're here to work on completing are seeded in our consciousness.

Divinely Inspired Programming

It turns out that unresolved issues are programmed into the software package of your consciousness even before you're old enough to consciously distinguish one thing from another. Before you developed the capacity to reason, you've made associations based upon your spiritually inspired predispositions. You behave the way you do not because of genetics or environmental influence, but rather because you came in *wired* to develop in that way. Consider the possibility that rather than *causing* the challenges you face in life, your genetics and environment *support* the spiritual agenda you're here to fulfill. So what are these "interpretations" you're prone to make? And how do you make them?

When we get inside an individual's consciousness, we find something astonishing. There's often an early-childhood experience, followed by an *interpretation* of that experience, which functioned as a defining moment. At such times, a conclusion is reached about the way things are (definition of reality), and a decision is made about how to behave in order to survive and cope in a world where these sorts of things occur. Frequently, these early *interpretations,* and the subsequent behavioral choices, set the tone for lifelong patterns.

For example, if an infant *perceived* she wasn't sufficiently held and cuddled at birth, she may have *interpreted* that experience to mean she was unwanted. Even if it were accurate that she was unwanted by her parents, from the vantage point of the individual's spiritual curriculum, that circumstance of birth could be seen as the way in which a pattern of unworthiness was seeded in her consciousness. In other words, whether a child is wanted or not is, from the Soul's perspective, independent of how that Soul will *interpret* its early experience. The Soul will choose in accordance with its spiritual curriculum.

We have found that if we can get *between* the experience and what the child decided about the experience based on his or her predisposition toward certain interpretations, we can begin the healing process. Why? *Because it's the interpretation one gives to experience that's really at issue.*

Said another way, *the core of healing involves a recontextualizing process through which people evolve to the place where they're <u>Seeing Through Soul-Centered Eyes.</u> In so doing, they actually redefine their reality by learning to choose interpretations more in alignment with a Soul-Centered context. The result is an enhanced sense of Self-Compassion and a higher level of consciousness.* This is true healing. We'll be taking you through a step-by-step healing process that utilizes this contextual understanding a few chapters from now.

The ramifications of such a process are not only radical but also far-reaching. Consider, for example, the implications for a public-school system that would seek to require every child to learn the same lessons regardless of each Soul's curriculum. It was precisely in response to this state of affairs that educators such as Maria Montessori and Rudolf Steiner founded their respective schools. They both had in common a dedication to providing an individual educational curriculum tailor-made to honor and support each child's Soul-directed uniqueness.

If what we're suggesting has validity, it would appear to lead into the philosophy of reincarnation. But does believing in re-incarnation or not really matter? Sometime ago, a wonderful inter-view with Dr. Ian Stevenson appeared in *The New York Times*. Dr. Stevenson was then the Director of the Department of Personality Studies at the University of Virginia. He had spent the better part of his life on evidence-gathering trips to check out the accuracy of people's claims of past-life memories.

(As a sidebar, while writing this I remembered part of an early conversation I had with Dr. Hunter when I questioned her about the existence of so-called past lives. She simply said, "Don't be concerned about it. You didn't believe it in your last life either.")

Some of Stevenson's fascinating results can be found in his work *Twenty Cases Suggestive of Reincarnation*. What was most nota-ble about the book, however, was not the nature of the evidence, but rather Dr. Stevenson's response to the question: "If reincarna-tion were widely accepted, how would it change the world?"

He answered:

> It would lessen guilt on the part of parents. They wouldn't have as much of a burden that, whatever goes wrong with a child is all their fault, either through genes or mishandling dur-ing the child's infancy. People themselves would have to take more responsibility for their own destinies. . . .

Wow! Now that's empowerment!

And then he added a most remarkable statement:

> I don't expect any great moral transformation. On my first trip to India I met a respected Indian monk, a swami. I told him I had come out to see what evidence there was in India for reincarnation. He remained silent for a long, long time. Then he said, "We here in India regard it as a fact that people are reborn,

but, you see, it doesn't make a difference because we have just as many rogues and villains in India as you have in the West."

Freedom and Personal Responsibility

The important thing is that, regardless of the mechanism a Soul uses to bring forward its curriculum, it's your individual responsibility to heal, resolve, or complete that pattern. To be successful in such an endeavor, the *willingness to assume personal responsibility* is the cornerstone, and that leads to the following principle:

> **Principle #13:** *Personal responsibility is the foundational key that opens the door to Freedom.*

The ego would scoff, "Nonsense! You can only be responsible for what's under your control. When things not under your control happen to you, obviously you're a victim of them. Individual suffering is caused by external circumstances."

The Authentic Self would gently and lovingly reply, "Regardless of what situations or circumstances you find yourself in, you're always responsible for the way you choose to respond to them."

I remember my doctoral-dissertation oral defense as if it were yesterday. (By the way, isn't it interesting that it's called a *defense?*) The five faculty members whose job it was to intellectually attack my position and mercilessly probe for chinks in my academic armor were seated across the table. I can still see them brandishing their mental sabers while I—outnumbered as I was by these superior, authoritative forces—could only rely upon the thoroughness of my training stemming from my total immersion in my chosen subject matter: *values.*

I don't recall how it came up, but I made this statement: "Freedom is often assumed to mean that we can do whatever we want whenever we want to do it." It was met not with a clash of steel, but rather with an incredulous lowering of blades and a quizzical, "What? Are you saying it's not?" Without realizing it, I had inadvertently stumbled upon their vulnerability by presenting a new way of looking at an idea. My *defense* was over. In that moment, we had become colleagues exploring the meaning of freedom.

From a Soul's vantage point, freedom has little to do with choices we make in physical-world reality. The Soul doesn't care if we take this road or that one, because it will use either road for its purposes of learning and healing. Freedom isn't about freedom *to,* but rather freedom *from.* In this sense it has much more to do with freedom *from* inner disturbance, independent of outside circumstances. *It is freedom from the bondage of unresolved issues. It is freedom from what we refer to as unnecessary emotional suffering.*

And yet, paradoxically, it's your choices that determine the quality of your life. Stephen R. Covey went right to the point when he wrote: "Until a person can say deeply and honestly, 'I am what I am today because of the choices I made yesterday,' that person cannot say, 'I choose otherwise.'"

Freedom is only possible when you enter into a willingness to take personal responsibility. Until you're willing to consider how the choices you're making contribute to your drama and suffering, you're involved in the plight of the victim, and you will report the situations in your life from the victim's perspective. As long as you insist upon blaming sources outside yourself for your circumstances and ensuing disturbances, you will maintain yourself in a victim position and will suffer accordingly.

But the moment you choose to accept personal responsibility for *all* your inner experiences *independent of what appears to have caused them,* the escape hatch *automatically* swings open, providing you with the opportunity for passing into the land of freedom. You become authentically empowered, and you discover there really is a calm at the center of the fiercest hurricane where you can reside. In fact, eventually you realize that you *are* that calm.

The willingness to take personal responsibility for everything in your consciousness is an essential component of Spiritual Psychology. There can be no exceptions. Taking responsibility seems like risky business and not at all attractive to the ego, for it involves the ego honestly looking at the times it may have contributed to the current predicament or dilemma. The ego hates doing this because, living in a dualistic reality, that would mean that it might have to admit that it was, dare we say it . . . *wrong.*

In this regard, courage is the coin you most require in your purse, for it seems to your physically oriented ego that by taking personal responsibility, you are drawing arbitrary lines in the sand by which you may be judged as wrong. You are essentially saying, "The buck stops here!"

It takes great courage to accept personal responsibility, for when this idea is heard for the first time, one of two things might happen inside: (1) Your ego will say, "What a ridiculous idea—a good example of misguided, woo-woo, New Age nonsense!" or (2) you may be ready to consider the possibility that somewhere inside you're open to having a different experience. You may have that exciting Aha! experience that resonates as a truer *truth* than your previous truth. And the next new awareness may replace the new truth you just learned with an even newer truth, and so on. As you continue awakening, your awareness of *truth* evolves to the point where you observe life *only* through Soul-Centered Eyes, and you realize that truth and Love mean the same thing: that Truth *is* Love, and Love *is* what is True.

Once you begin processing life in this exciting new way, you begin moving into the full-responsibility mode. It's here that our next principle is found:

Principle #14: *Nothing outside of you causes your disturbances.*

There are no exceptions to this principle and no avoiding it. You can either do "I am upset because . . ." or you can do "I am 100 percent responsible for any disturbance going on in my consciousness regardless of what seems to have triggered it." There's no such thing as in between, and the choice is always yours. Always!

Notice that we're not saying: "I am responsible for anything and everything going on outside of my life." While, to a greater or lesser degree, you may have *influence* over many of the events occurring in your life, rarely, if ever, do you actually have *control* over anything happening outside yourself. However, you do have dominion over everything going on within your consciousness, and this is where true empowerment is found.

From within this position of personal responsibility, you're essentially saying that no matter what goes on outside, you have the power and clarity to stay in balance and at Peace. And when you don't, you can recognize that your school is in session and work on healing the part inside that's disturbed. But you can't have it both ways. You can't be willing to take responsibility for your disturbance *except* when something has happened about which there really is good reason to be upset. Yes, we are suggesting that there *really* is no such thing as a good reason to be upset.

You can play the victim role or the empowered role, but you can't play both simultaneously any more than someone can be pregnant and not pregnant at the same time. It's only when you're willing to claim 100 percent responsibility for your internal process, regardless of how good the reasons are for blaming others, that you have any chance whatsoever of completing your Soul-orchestrated curriculum. Prior to that time, you'll continue as if gains in the physical world are what life is all about.

Humanity will probably continue at its rapid technological pace and arrive at a time when, like Captain Kirk and the *Enterprise* crew, we'll have a Scotty to beam us up. However, regardless of how much external-world technological progress we make, we'll still find that no matter where we go, there we are. For technological progress in itself will never fulfill our Souls' desire and destiny . . . which is to beam up into the waiting arms of God.

Soul-Centered Practices

The domain of responsibility is both crucial and very interesting in that it operates on both the Goal and Learning Lines of Life. For that reason, we have two practices, one for each context. Let's start with *Facilitating Responsibility I: Choice,* which functions primarily on the Goal Line.

Facilitating Responsibility I: Choice

What can make taking personal responsibility challenging is that the word *responsibility,* in Western culture, often has a sense of obligation or burden associated with it. Many people think the following: "If I find that I have responsibility for a certain situation or feeling, then that means I'm obligated to do something about it." But the word simply means the ability to respond, and you always have a choice in how you do this: You can choose to continue responding to something the way you have been, or you can decide on another course of action. It's up to you.

What also can make taking personal responsibility challenging is a reluctance to evaluate your choices because you don't want to be blamed or blame yourself for poor ones. It's the ego's right/wrong model. The Authentic Self isn't concerned with right and wrong. It's only concerned with learning, and utilizes the *evaluative* or *What works better?* approach to life. So if your intention is to live from within a Soul-Centered context, what you want to do is accept what *is* without judgment, take 100 percent responsibility for your choices, and begin making more positive choices. After all, one really good definition of insanity is doing the same thing over and over expecting a different result.

For this exercise it's also important to recognize that the word *responsibility* is often paired with the word *commitment.* Making that connection is a mistake in that it will tend to limit your willingness to consider other choices that may be more productive. So when you engage in the following process, please divorce these two concepts from each other. All you want to do is consider the possibility of other choices. It's not necessary for you to commit to doing anything different at this time. We are simply asking you to consider other options. When you do the process, we think you'll see what we mean.

1. Center your awareness in your heart and consciously look for the Loving Essence within. Allow yourself to identify a current situation that you would like to be different.

Example: I've wanted to write a children's book for some time now, but I don't ever seem to get around to starting it.

2. Are you aware of any choices (inner and/or outer) you're presently making that tend to maintain the situation as it is?

Example: Well, inwardly I'm aware that when I think of writing, I tell myself that what I have to say isn't really very important anyway. And outwardly I choose to do other things, the result of which is that I put off writing until some future unspecified time.

3. Take your time and consider the possibility of other choices that might produce different results. It's not that you have to do anything differently; can you simply see any alternatives?

Example: Inwardly, I could choose to tell myself that what I want to share is valuable and worthwhile, and outwardly, of course, I could choose to schedule some specific time to sit down and write.

4. Without committing to doing anything different at this time, take a few minutes and visualize yourself in the process of making the new choices in the present, as if you were making them now.

Example: Here I am, sitting at my desk. I'm aware of the impulse inside of myself to write a beautiful children's book. I'm choosing to honor that impulse, and I've scheduled two hours in the morning, four days a week, for writing. And here I am happily writing, and the words are just pouring out of me. I feel wonderful.

Do you notice any difference in your awareness? Many people perceive a subtle shift in their consciousness just from doing this visualization once.

Our experience has shown us that doing Step 4—visualizing yourself engaging in the new behavior—daily for a minimum of 32 consecutive days often results in extraordinary shifts in a person's behavior. In case you're wondering why we use 32 days, there's something powerful about going beyond a typical month of 30 or 31 days that serves to anchor a new behavior pattern in consciousness. We recommend creating a calendar with 32 boxes, starting with the date you begin. So if June 5 happens to fall on a Tuesday, that would be day one and you'd build the calendar from there. June 6 would be day two, and so on. The best time for most people to do this short process seems to be in the evening just prior to going to sleep. In fact, many find it helpful to keep the calendar on their pillows as a reminder to do the process. Then, in the morning, they place a check in the box representing the previous evening. It doesn't have to take more than a few minutes each time, and we believe you'll find the results well worth the effort.

Facilitating Responsibility II: Ownership

This practice functions primarily on the Learning Line. While the first aspect of *responsibility* has to do with simply giving yourself permission to see new possibilities for choices you're currently making, the second has to do with the willingness to take 100 percent *responsibility* for what's going on within your own consciousness. Moving into such willingness can be extremely challenging, as well as extremely empowering. It can be challenging since once you dare to look, you run the risk of entering into self-blame or self-recrimination. Believe it or not, we've heard there's even a name for it—New Age guilt!

Once the notion of personal responsibility became more widespread, some people began taking it in a direction it was never intended to go. Their reasoning went something like this: "What? Are you saying that I'm responsible for everything that goes on in my life? You mean I'm responsible for my cancer? Oh my God, why would I do such a terrible thing to myself? Why would I cause myself so much pain and suffering? This is even more evidence of what an unworthy person I am." Can you see how the ego is using the potentially liberating Principle #12 *(unresolved issues are not bad;*

they are just part of your spiritual curriculum and are an opportunity for healing) and turning it back on itself to maintain its original position of unworthiness? In other words, there's a temptation to take what has happened and use it as *proof of your unworthiness* rather than as an indicator that you likely have inner work to do regarding your reaction to whatever has happened.

What's the alternative? Within the spiritual context, you'd assume that you're responsible for everything in your life. However, you usually don't know the spiritual reason why your Soul would choose an experience such as cancer. What you do know is that all of life serves a spiritual purpose, and since illness is a part of life, cancer must serve one, too.

The question of purpose aside, *Facilitating Responsibility II: Ownership* allows you to move into a space where you're essentially saying, "Regardless of what I am working with, I am 100 percent *responsible* for my internal reality. I am *responsible* for my attitudes, what I tell myself about my experience, and how I choose to deal with it. And I'm especially responsible for any negativity I'm running inside myself that supports an 'I am upset because . . .' position. My intention is simply to accept what's present and not make myself, or my experience, wrong."

In summary, you must be willing to take individual responsibility for any disturbance you experience. Again, this is a four-step process:

1. Center your awareness in your heart and consciously look for the Loving Essence within. Allow yourself to identify a recent experience where you found yourself experiencing emotional distress and wanting to blame yourself or someone else for what happened and for your reaction.

> *Example:* I've wanted to write a children's book for some time, but I don't ever seem to get around to starting it. I tell myself that what I have to say isn't really very important or valuable anyway, and then I get upset because I keep procrastinating.

2. Utilizing the Soul-Centered Practices of *Seeing the Loving Essence* and *Heart-Centered Listening,* and without trying to change anything, allow yourself to move into a place of Acceptance: Acceptance of what is; of your feelings; of your actions; and even of any conclusions you may have drawn about yourself, others, and/or your experience.

> *Example:* I'm learning that the nature of God is Love and that since I'm a part of God, my nature is also Love. I don't have to like my feelings or my actions in order to accept them. I can simply accept them for what they are. In fact, that's the most Loving and liberating thing I can do.

3. Once you've entered a place of Acceptance, allow yourself to accept ownership of your feelings and actions without blaming anyone, especially yourself. Remember that no matter what you did, how you felt at the time, or how you're feeling right now, you're still a beautiful, valuable, and lovable Soul who's truly doing your best.

> *Example:* I can see that I don't have to make anyone wrong, including myself, for my feelings and actions. I can also see that by accepting responsibility for my feelings and actions I'm free to work on changing them. I'm no longer a victim of what's happening outside myself.

4. Gently remind yourself that anytime you feel upset, all that has happened is that your spiritual agenda is revealing places in your consciousness that are in need of healing, and that these situations are God-given opportunities for progressing spiritually.

> *Example:* I recognize that this entire situation is pointing out to me a place where I have work to do regarding my own sense of unworthiness and lack of value. And when I choose to accept responsibility for the situation and my inner process, I have a tremendous feeling of empowerment.

When you've completed *Facilitating Responsibility II: Ownership,* you may experience a sense of incompletion. You may be thinking,

Okay, I can accept my feelings and actions, but now what? What can I do with that awareness? It's helpful to understand that this is a door-opening process. Think of a baseball game: This Soul-Centered Practice is a mechanism that allows you to move from the stadium of spectators onto the field of play. You receive a bat, step up to the plate, and have the opportunity to hit a home run. Until such time, you remain a spectator. Later in the book, we'll introduce you to a process that you can use to hit home runs—sometimes with the bases loaded!

Facilitating Responsibility II: Ownership is another one of the processes that lends itself to a 32-day strategy like the one we described following *Facilitating Responsibility I: Choice*. Both of these processes often result in significant shifts in consciousness. Of course, there's only one way for you to find out how significant they may be for you: try them!

⁰⁄ᴐ⁰⁄ᴐ

Stem Sentences to Write Down and Contemplate

- If what happens outside myself doesn't *cause* me to be upset, but merely triggers upset already present in my consciousness, then . . .

- And if what happens outside myself doesn't *cause* me to be happy, but merely triggers happiness already present in my consciousness, then . . .

- If I am truly willing to take 100 percent personal responsibility for *everything* that goes on in my inner awareness, with no exceptions, then . . .

- If unresolved issues are not bad, then . . .

- If unresolved issues are part of my spiritual curriculum, then . . .

- I'm not so sure that I'm ready to let go of blaming _____ for . . .

Repeat as often as necessary.

CHAPTER SIX

MEET THE STACKERS

Some people help us, and some seem to hinder us.
When seen through Soul-Centered Eyes, they all serve
to assist us in accomplishing our Spiritual purpose.

Among the great mysteries of life, the notion of time ranks right up near the top. What is this stuff called time anyway? We seem to exist in it with the same certainty that air we breath sustains our lives. We take time as a given because it's so obviously visible in the changes we see in a single day and over a lifetime.

Like air, time appears to be subject to scientific verification, since we have ways of measuring it. But, experientially, what exactly *is* it?

Most of us have learned to view time as an unimaginably long continuum that began with the big bang some 14 billion years ago, give or take a billion. Since then, what is referred to as Creation has unfolded through time to bring us to this present moment—and then on to the next moment and the one after that—as time rushes like a river on its endless journey through eternity.

People speak of everything using *now* as a reference point and have named the direction of what's already happened as the *past* and what is yet to happen as the *future,* as if by doing so we've somehow gained a degree of control over the dimension itself. Further, we've been conditioned to believe that time is constant, or standing still, and we are moving through *it.* We even have devices called clocks that tell us precisely where we are on this eternal progression.

In other words, there exists a perception of time that humankind has agreed upon. This way of defining it is a mental function that references events in the physical world as past, present, and future. Since all of this occurs within the fabric of the mind, it's the ego that's involved in constructing the apparent continuum. Even feelings are referenced in time, as they're associated with something that has happened, is happening, or may happen. And the majority of humanity accepts this paradigm as constructed by historians and futurists. After all, this system works very well in physical-world reality. Trains and planes depart and arrive according to a schedule (sometimes), and restaurant reservations are more easily managed if we determine at what hour we'll dine. The following diagram is a visual representation of this dynamic:

Figure 10

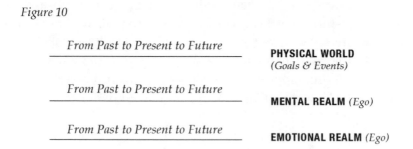

However, from studies in physics, it's well known that many of the beliefs about time we grew up with are actually naïve. Time, like all else that exists in the universe, can only be understood in relation to everything else. Physicists have proven that time is not constant, nor does it have the same measure in all situations. For example, verified experiments have demonstrated that synchronized clocks don't always gauge time at the same rate; further, what they register is greatly influenced by the *frame of reference* of the observer.

The movie we think best conveys this awareness of the inconsistency of time is *Contact*, which is about a research scientist involved with an unusual-looking spacecraft constructed for the purpose of intergalactic travel. She travels through a series of wormholes to a distant planet. There, she converses with a resident being, and then returns home again within an 18-hour period. However, those on Earth monitoring the liftoff only observe and record the craft falling for six seconds into a safety net, apparently going nowhere. For the space traveler, six seconds of Earth time equated to 18 hours of interstellar time. Whose experience is valid? In the film, the fact that the ship records 18 hours of static during those six seconds of Earth time is purposely hidden from the public. How interesting . . .

The time phenomenon in the film is similar to most people's personal subjective experience of time, which varies greatly according to circumstances. Time flies when you're having fun, drags if you're feeling bored, and seems to stand still in a moment of crisis. In a deep meditative state, you may experience a sense of timelessness as you enter the infinite expanse of what has been called the *eternal now.*

Regardless of the physical nature of time, our focus in Spiritual Psychology involves the role time plays in the dimension of personal experiential reality.

If you were asked, "What time is it?" what would you answer? Would you look at your wristwatch and report what you read on its face? And if you did, would your answer be the definition of what time is at that precise moment? Obviously not, since at the exact same moment, the answer will be different for anyone in another time zone. In fact, if you'd like some mental exercise, try calculating the time in, say, Sydney, Australia, or Oslo, Norway, while looking at your watch in New York City.

In fact, experientially speaking, the only answer you can ever truly give that's accurate everywhere on the planet at the same instant is "Now!" No matter where you are, it's never a week from now and it's never a week ago. It's always *now!* The only time that exists experientially is *now!* As someone once said, "The illusion of time is God's way of assuring that everything doesn't happen all at once."

Those who meditate often experience a slowing of their breathing. At such times, they frequently report reaching a place of rest in which they feel themselves moving out of the dimension of time altogether into what was described earlier as an eternal now. The best layperson's description of the process we've ever read is found in Itzhak Bentov's work in which he describes the arc of a pendulum as coming to a place at the end of a swing in either direction where it's neither moving one way or the other. For an immeasurable instant, it's at rest. In our model of consciousness, what we're saying would look like this:

Figure 11

From Past to Present to Future	**PHYSICAL REALM** *(Goals & Events)*
From Past to Present to Future	**MENTAL REALM** *(Ego)*
From Past to Present to Future	**EMOTIONAL REALM** *(Ego)*
NOW • TIMELESS • ALWAYS	**AUTHENTIC SELF**

Who's in Charge of Now?

If the only real time in the context of human experience is *now,* we're faced with a very unusual challenge in perspective. Rather than time standing still and us moving through it, it's more accurate to say that *we* are standing still and what we call time is moving through *now.* It's we who are in reality, and time is the changing variable.

So let's assume that you're standing still in the midst of *now.* If you could look into the dimension of time, what would you see? There would appear a series of events stacked up like this: Those that have already happened, which is called the past, would be seen as moving away from *now* in one direction; and in the other, which is called the future, would be a lineup of probable events patiently waiting their turn to come into manifestation *now.* In other words, experientially speaking, you aren't going through time—time is going through *now.*

Figure 12

DISTANT PAST ← PAST ← NOW ← FUTURE ← DISTANT FUTURE

People with well-developed clairvoyant abilities can foresee these potential future events stacked up waiting to appear in someone's life *now*. The challenge such individuals often have is in pinpointing the specific time when a certain incident is set to occur. It's simply queued up without a time stamp. Absent of such references, clairvoyants utilize clues, such as how old someone looks in the inner pictures they see, to estimate the time frame. Of course, just because an event is foreseen doesn't mean that it will actually take place. The future that's perceived by an intuitive may simply be symbolic—carrying a message, as in a dream. Or it might have a high probability of happening in physical reality unless a shift takes place between now and then that alters the current trajectory of one's life.

Seeing into the realm of future possibilities is a lot like viewing the coming attractions in a movie theater. You're shown some of the scenes you'll see if you attend this particular film. However, you won't see any of them if you choose a different movie. *Choice* is the key word here, and that's where the freedom to choose comes into play. And sometimes the only choice is your attitude. In fact, it's often precisely through a shift in attitude that you effect a profound change in your life. In other words, you can often alter your experience by changing your point of view.

Imagine what it would take if you found yourself in a concentration camp, as Viktor Frankl described in his inspiring book *Man's Search for Meaning*. Consider where you would have had to arrive in your consciousness for you to conclude from your experience, like Frankl did: "Everything can be taken from [someone] but one thing: the last of the human freedoms—to choose one's attitude in any given set of circumstances, to choose one's own way."

Once you recognize the possibility that the future events of your life are waiting in line to "strut and fret" their "hour upon the stage," you become much less interested in finding out what those events might be and much more so in discovering *who* is writing, directing, and producing the play.

You eventually come to a particular perspective that you have found helps you accept your experiences with greater neutrality and equanimity. At the same time, this viewing point empowers you to take the action or make the shifts that will support you in creating a more fulfilling life.

If you're willing to consider the possibility of a queue of probable events moving into your experience one at a time, the important questions are: *Who determines the lineup?* and *How is it that a particular kind of event seems to occur with greater frequency than others?*

Consider the possibility that you have spiritual allies who *stack up* potential events in accordance with your Earth School curriculum or karma and then send them to you at opportune moments in support of your spiritual growth. Since these helpers are in charge of the stack of experiences queued up in the field of possibilities, let's simply call them *the Stackers.*

A Stacker's Job is Never Done

We look upon the Stackers as instruments of the Soul—the overall conductors of everyone's life. The music they play is written by the choices we've all made, often in the distant past. And the grace with which we dance to this music enables us to even the score (no pun intended), and even change the tune.

The Stackers operate on life's Learning Line. Some of the Goal Line events they send you might appear favorable, and others may be potentially disastrous—especially initially. What they all have in common is that they provide you with learning opportunities consistent with your Soul's curriculum.

Remember, the Soul doesn't judge these experiences as good or bad. It knows, as do the Stackers, that after your "hour upon the stage"—no matter how glorious or tumultuous it may have been— you will return to your Home in Wholeness, or Holiness, with a greater depth of Wisdom, Compassion, and Understanding, having used your experiences in service to your spiritual evolution.

Of course, no one rejoices in hardship when it comes. But as Emerson so eloquently put it, "Our strength grows out of our weakness. Not until we are pricked and stung and sorely shot at, awakens the indignation which arms itself with secret forces."

Often the most admired people are those who have demonstrated that even the greatest challenge, tragedy, or injustice can eventually bear life-nourishing spiritual fruit, as evidenced by individuals such as Mother Teresa, Abraham Lincoln, and Nelson Mandela. Difficult circumstances can impel you on an inward journey that deepens your conscious connection with your essential Self. They also can open your eyes to a greater purpose in life, enhance your compassionate connection with others, and enable you to be of greater service in the world. "For everything you have missed, you have gained something else," Emerson wrote. "And for everything you gain, you lose something."

Within the context of Spiritual Psychology, your life experiences collectively provide continual opportunities for learning the lessons of your spiritual curriculum. And (time to breathe a big sigh of relief) everyone is destined to graduate from the Earth School. It really is just a matter of time, so to speak. And since the only time is *now,* you may as well get busy with your spiritual work, which is always available via the experiences at hand.

Your ego, of course, would disagree. From within the dualistic framework of seeing things, you tend to define upcoming events as *good* or *bad, blessings* or *curses.* But when viewed from a higher perspective, events themselves are neutral. They aren't set up for punishment, success, or failure. They're set up for learning! Here's an example.

A Challenge from Our Stackers

Several years ago, we were vacationing in the beautiful Lake District in England and were driving to meet with a group who was to spend five days together sharing inspirational poetry in the morning, hiking in the afternoon, and trying out some local pubs in the evening. We were anticipating a lovely time.

If you've ever driven in that part of the world, you know that the roads are very narrow and often quite windy due to the hilly landscape. And it certainly doesn't make things easier when you're driving a rented vehicle, you're on the "wrong" side of the road in unfamiliar terrain, and it's raining.

All of a sudden, I accidentally drove our rental car over a large nail and the left front tire blew out. The first thing we had to contend with was the narrowness of the road that had no shoulder. Fortunately, we noticed a rare dirt area on the right-hand side and pulled onto it. This feat was not as easy as it sounds, since driving on the left side of the road, as they do in England, meant driving across the lane of possible oncoming traffic. Thankfully, there wasn't any.

We got out of the car and looked at the tire, and I said to Mary, "Wow, that was amazing. Thank God we're okay and didn't get into an accident." Then, as if making a fantastic proclamation, I said, "It's flat! Great! We're going to be late. We'd best call and let them know. Do you have your cell phone handy?"

"Sure!" She quickly found it and attempted to dial. "Looks like we don't have any reception here."

I pulled out my phone. No luck. "Wonderful! I'm so glad we made all that effort to get international phone numbers. Now what?" I could feel myself starting to move into the "poor me" victim role.

To my surprise, Mary looked at me, smiled, and then began to laugh. "I think I know what's going on here. This is obviously a setup compliments of the Stackers." She went on, "I don't like this any more than you do. And we both have a choice in how we respond to this situation. Let's accept what is—no AAA to rescue us—and get on with changing the tire."

"In this weather?" I replied incredulously. "That would mean unloading all the suitcases from the trunk and standing them in the rain to get at the spare. And besides, this is a rental car, and I'm not sure how to use the jack."

She shrugged. "It's either changing the tire or hiking in the rain to the nearest phone, and who knows how far that is."

"So if I'm hearing you correctly, you're suggesting we unload all the luggage in the rain and *have fun* changing the tire. Have I got it?"

"You've got it," she said, with all the confidence that comes with knowing full well she wouldn't be the one unloading the luggage or changing the tire. At that prospect, I too started laughing. "Very funny. Okay, I'm in."

So I unloaded the mountain of suitcases and located the spare tire and jack. I noticed another odd wrench whose purpose was a mystery to me, so I left it where it was. I also noticed that the jack had the lug-nut wrench at its opposite end, so I took the jack and spare over to the flat. Little did we know part two of our test was about to begin.

As I began to ratchet up the left front of the car, I noticed that there was a lock on one of the lug nuts, which secured the tire to the wheel. It being a rental car, each wheel was equipped with this theft-protection device.

"Mary, look at this! I don't believe it! I have no idea how to get this lock off the wheel."

Upon seeing this turn of events, Mary began laughing even harder, and so did I. "Hey," she said, "how about we look in the owner's manual?"

"What a great idea! Do you know where it is?"

"No, do you?"

By this time, we were close to hysterics as we located the manual in the glove box. Sure enough, there were the instructions, and guess what—the mystery tool that I initially left in the trunk turned out to be the wrench that unlocked the lug nuts.

The rest of the tire-changing process went pretty smoothly. After loading the luggage back in the trunk, off we went.

As a sidebar, a flat tire is precisely the example we use in class when we present the Stackers talk. For us, it was clearly a time for testing. Think about it. Here we were on a remote road in the north of England with a flat tire, no cell-phone service, no AAA, a car we were clueless about, a spare tire buried in a trunk full of luggage, an antitheft lock on the tire we needed to change—*and* it was raining, and our rain gear was neatly packed away in one of the suitcases. What a fabulous *reason* to move into a justified and righteous "I am upset because . . ." attitude.

As we drove, we imagined our Stackers sitting back (if they have chairs in those realms) and evaluating how we handled the situation. They knew that there were basically two choices, with many variations in between:

1. The first choice would have been for one or both of us to get triggered and move into "I am upset because the tire is flat, and we're going to be late, and we have no cell-phone reception, and it's raining, and our rain gear is packed away, and the tire is locked, and we don't know how to change it," and so on. If we reacted from this victim stance, we probably would become extremely upset, with escalating heart rates and blood pressure to match. We might even move into judgment with an "I am upset because . . ." attitude that would quickly degenerate into unkindness and blaming each other. Perhaps we've all experienced that to some degree. It's not a great way to create magical, memorable moments together.

If this first approach were chosen, the Stackers would compassionately confer and conclude something like: "It doesn't seem as though they're getting it. We better stack up ten more similar events so they'll have ample opportunity for mastering 'I am upset because . . .' After all, they teach this stuff."

2. The second choice would be to move into Acceptance and simply respond with equanimity while doing whatever was necessary. Once we could safely get to the side of the road and catch our breath, we could get out of the car, recognize the opportunity present on the Learning Line, and move into Acceptance. In this case our heart rates and blood pressure would remain where they were prior to the flat tire. And if we chose this response, the Stackers would know we'd probably be grateful for our safety and then go about handling the Goal Line situation in a neutral, balanced way. And if this happened, they would high-five each other and say, "All right! Looks like they're getting it. Let's take off ten similar events."

That's a pretty accurate description of the way to create your future. If your Soul's purpose on Earth is to support you in awakening more fully into the reality of your spiritual nature, doesn't it make sense that your learning would be competency based? It's really no different from when you were a kid learning to spell. When you demonstrated that you could correctly spell all the words on one list, you'd progress to the next. By the inner and outer choices you make *now,* you instruct the Stackers regarding what sorts of experiences to line up for your ongoing growth and learning.

This realization alone is potentially life changing and leads to the next two principles:

Principle #15: *You create your future by how you respond to experiences* <u>*now.*</u>

Principle #16: *How you relate to an issue* <u>*is*</u> *the issue, and how you relate to yourself while you go through an issue* <u>*is*</u> *the issue.*

The good news is that, in many instances, you can and do actually change your stacked-up future. Because what will happen is largely dependent upon how you handle things in your *now,* there's no rule that an event currently waiting to come in must actually manifest. Until it emerges into *now,* it exists only as a potential with a probability of occurrence. Your very next choice can alter the entire lineup. As the Chinese proverb instructs us, "All the flowers of all the tomorrows are planted in the seeds of today."

Recognizing a Test from Your Stackers

The Stackers aren't invested in the kinds of experiences you have. They understand that it's largely up to you, and they cooperate fully. Their job is to support you in the process of spiritually awakening, independent of ramifications in the physical world.

Over the years, we've seen that the more people learn to make choices in alignment with their Loving nature, the more life seems to smooth out and the less they seem to have to deal with experiences they'd prefer not to. And when challenges do occur, they're more conscious, resilient, and effective in responding to them.

Another interesting job the Stackers have is to keep track of all your previous choices. And even when you've demonstrated mastery over parts of your curriculum, every now and then they'll set up one of those old used-to-trigger-distress experiences just to check that you've truly mastered the learning.

Speaking of Stackers, I had a dream a while back that I was standing in a kitchen. Known far and wide to be one of my Stackers' most effective agents, my mother stood right behind me and peered over my shoulder as I chopped vegetables on a wooden cutting board. As I cut, she kept saying that I wasn't doing it right, that I should do it differently, and what was wrong with me anyway? In the dream, I was inwardly aware of the learning opportunity and told myself, *This is a test. Stay neutral!* Nevertheless, she continued to criticize me relentlessly.

Despite my best efforts, the anger started rising in my solar plexus. Finally, I lost my cool, wheeled around, and—wielding my knife like a saber—snapped, "What's the matter with you? I've been chopping vegetables for years. I know how to chop vegetables. Can't you just let me cut the vegetables the way I want to cut them?"

She took a step back, smiled at me, and with a peculiar tilt of her head and short jab with her pointer finger, said, "Gotcha!" I immediately woke up, and hopefully before the Stackers could say, "Tack on ten more," I started working with myself to release the judgment I had just issued.

In that dream, I didn't pass the test. I was shown that I had more inner work to do in the area pertaining to anger (at least when it came to my mother). In a way, one could say that life continually presents us with tests and learning opportunities, all potential vehicles for spiritual evolution. As USM's founder and chancellor, John-Roger, has said:

> Tests are not necessarily tribulations. They are areas of revelation. Tests are for you to reveal unto **yourself** where you have to work and what you have to do. You can say, "This is neat," and go toward it and clear it. You can't get away from it so you might just as well go toward it and clear it. Or, if it

can't be cleared immediately, maybe you're to learn patience or experience a certain level to learn compassion. There are many possibilities. And all you have to do in any situation is use it to direct yourself in a positive consciousness.

Here's a sure way to know whether something is a lesson or a test: If you passed, it was a test. If not, it was a lesson, and more will be coming.

How do you know when you've attained such mastery? A really good answer to this question can be found in Richard Bach's classic book *Illusions*. He sounds just like a Stacker when he writes: "Here is a test to find whether your mission on earth is finished: If you're alive, it isn't." From the altitude of higher consciousness, it's like that wonderful song "From a Distance," in which Bette Midler sings in the refrain that God is watching us.

And, of course, none of this work goes on in the past or the future. All of it only happens *now*. How you deal with every life situation *now* is of paramount importance in determining future situations. If you say that you'll choose differently later, after such and such has happened, all you're really saying is that you're not ready to face whatever it is you have the opportunity to address *now*.

We don't know about you, but we're clear that the name of the game is to learn how to walk through the rest of this lifetime with as much Acceptance, Kindness, Compassion, and Joy as possible. Our intention is to heal as many unresolved issues as we can. We know that the more we can peel away or dissolve the restricting, conditioned patterns that mask who we truly are, the more we will see through Soul-Centered Eyes and realize our Loving nature. And, at the same time—and perhaps even more important—we want to learn how to make both inner and outer choices such that we don't create new limiting patterns as we go forward.

The key idea here is simple: experientially, there's no future and there's no past; there's only *now*. Of course, we'd heard for years how important it was to "live in the now." Haven't you? But it didn't make any sense until we considered it in the context of spiritual progression. If every choice we make is important in determining our future, we certainly want our Stackers to be saying about our choices what an old sorcerer said when his apprentice was facing the life-or-death test of choosing between an elixir and a poison. When the apprentice drank what he accurately perceived to be the healing potion, the sorcerer exclaimed, "He chose wisely."

Stem Sentences to Write Down and Contemplate

- If now is the only time that exists, then . . .
- Some of my Stackers include . . .
- Lessons my Stackers are helping me learn are . . .

Repeat as often as necessary.

CHAPTER SEVEN

It's Okay to Change Your Mind

Beliefs aren't really all that important. They only inform and determine the quality of your entire life.

Do you ever wonder how people change their minds? Or perhaps a better way to phrase the question is: when, or under what conditions, do people change their minds? (Really, people don't actually "change" their minds. What you can do is change the contents of your mind, and you do this by changing software—the programs or beliefs you have permitted to be installed and allow to continue running.)

In our line of work, these are vitally important questions, because the difference between peace and disturbance usually depends upon what thoughts, beliefs, attitudes, and definitions of reality are predominant in a person's mind.

Levels of Awareness

As Mary and I showed you in Chapter 4, there are three major levels of awareness we humans all experience inwardly: the mental and emotional levels; the conscious components of the ego; and the Authentic Self, which isn't a level per se, because it actually encompasses all awareness. It would be more accurate to say that the dualistic-oriented ego exists in its own version of reality within the all-encompassing Love of the Authentic Self.

In addition to these three levels, there's also an unconscious component of the ego, which we'll discuss in Chapter 10, and the physical world—the stage upon which the entire drama is played out. Now let's consider each of these levels through the lens of your ability to choose.

— In *physical-world reality,* you do get to choose your behaviors, and as you know only too well from all those broken New Year's resolutions, it's much easier to say you'll do something than to actually do it. While you do have choice on the physical level, it's not always that easy to exercise it.

— Let's look at the *emotional level.* Do you consciously choose your emotions? I'm afraid not! We call the emotional level the yo-yo realm. Sometimes the yo-yo is up, and sometimes it's down. Emotions seem to have a *mind* of their own.

Suppose we were to offer you a million dollars to fall in love with a randomly selected stranger. While you might give it a valiant try, you couldn't do it. It just doesn't work that way. We once pointed this out to someone, and he said, "Could I get a thousand for just kissing her?"

— How about the *unconscious?* Do you consciously choose what resides in your unconscious? Another no! If you did, it wouldn't be unconscious.

— What about the *Authentic Self?* Surely you must have a choice in what happens within the Authentic Self. Sorry! As we've said over and over again, all that ever goes on in the Authentic Self is Loving and its derivatives: Peace, Compassion, Acceptance, Enthusiasm, and Joy. Period!

— That leaves the *mind.* Don't you get to choose what's in your mind? At last, *yes!* You certainly do get to choose what you hold there. You get to choose your attitude, what you believe, what you value, and which thoughts you will ruminate on all day long. It's precisely because you have such relatively easy access to the mind and so little access to the other levels of awareness that the mind becomes a focus for much of the self-help work that's available today.

⚬⚬⚬

There are two main ways to work toward spiritual evolution.

1. The first is the time-honored method of engaging in practices designed to uplift yourself directly into the Authentic Self. Examples of such practices would include meditation, spiritual exercises, prayer, contemplation, acts of selfless service, time in Silence, experiences in nature, and even valor in times of war. Anything will work that has the effect of lifting you out of your ego and into the Love concordant with the Authentic Self.

2. The second is by working through the ego to release the barriers erected over the course of your spiritual existence. The construction of barriers is accomplished through the use of building blocks consisting of certain *beliefs* existing in the mind—specifically those resulting in emotional suffering. The better you get at *changing beliefs in a positive direction,* the more you will *automatically* lift into the Authentic Self, which has been patiently waiting all along. As Mary and I have said, spiritual awakening and evolution are more processes of unlearning, deconditioning, and/or relearning than of acquiring more knowledge.

Personally, we have been working with the two approaches for many years and are advocates of both. We can attest that utilizing the second method (changing beliefs that had previously resulted in emotional pain) has accelerated our spiritual development. And we know from experience that the process of dissolving self-created barriers allows us to see/know our Divinity. The good news is that the context and methodology for dissolving these walls are now available by utilizing the principles and practices of Spiritual Psychology. Said another way, *rapid spiritual advancement is now possible through the direct application of a healing process that supports you in completing the purposes for which you have come to the Earth School in the first place.*

Let's take a few moments and see just how powerful and flexible your mind can be and how you can use conscious choice to shift your reality. Imagine that you're in a 15' by 15' locked room, bound to a chair by ropes. About a foot away from you is a table upon which rests a loaded .45-caliber pistol, a knife with a hunting blade, and a sharp spear. Suddenly, the door swings open and in bound six hungry wolves that head straight for you. What would you do?

If your mind works like ours, you'll realize you have to act fast. How quickly can you retrieve the knife to cut the ropes so you can grab the gun? After a few seconds, you'll probably conclude that you don't have enough time to avoid becoming a lupine lunch.

But remember how we set this up? We said, "*Imagine* that you're in a 15' by 15' locked room . . ." Do you see it now? The way out is to stop imagining!

She Thought She Was Dead

If you think this a bit far-fetched, consider the following story from a USM grad, a physician who related an extraordinary experience with a patient in her practice.

The doctor and her patient had grown close over the decade they had worked together. Unfortunately, the patient suffered from a severe chronic infection that had grown progressively worse over time—it had gotten to the point that essentially all of the organs and systems in her body were affected. Here's how our former student described the events that developed:

> In recent weeks, my patient's thoughts had become confused; and shortly before Christmas, her troubled husband brought her into my office. His eyes were sad and hers were downcast. She'd decided that she was dead. She wasn't clear when exactly she thought she'd died, but she was *very* clear that she was no longer living. There was nothing metaphorical about our conversation. She was sure she had died and that no one else had noticed. Her family was devastated; her husband was at his wit's end. This usually peaceful woman was beside herself,

trying to reconcile the disparity between her perception and those of everyone around her . . . including mine.

No amount of reasoning could change this experience for her. She wasn't to be talked out of this by anyone. After three or four visits of what seemed to be rather futile conversations, I entered the examination room, where I observed the two of them glaring at each other. He was mad because she still thought she was dead. She was mad because he still thought she was alive. I had no idea how to mediate this one. I sat down and suddenly looked at both of them and remembered that USM time-honored adage: "How we relate to an issue *is* the issue."

And so I suggested to them both that it frankly didn't make any difference if she was dead or alive. The circumstances were that she was still here, on the earth, and that she might as well make the best of it as long as she was. She might as well go on eating, sleeping, collecting coins, and entertaining her grandchildren when they visited. She might as well talk to her husband about the ordinary events of their lives and just let her physical process take its own course in its own time.

The whole idea was appealing to her. She didn't have to worry about it anymore. She could just do whatever she was accustomed to doing, whether she was dead or alive. She smiled for the first time in weeks. He smiled for the first time in weeks. Her daughter called later, delighted with the fact that even though her mother was still certain she was dead, she was back to her "usual self." She had simply chosen a different way to relate to the issue.

Literature is replete with quotes that tell us that what goes on in our minds has a tremendous effect on our lives. Emerson said, "We are prisoners of ideas," and "A man is what he thinks about all day long."

No small matter is the mind, and no small effect flows from the quality of your mental experience. Because the mind is where you have the greatest amount of choice, it's here we direct your attention. It's here that you can gain a tremendous amount of leverage.

Rules Do a Prison Make

Have you ever noticed that when something you don't like happens, you often react by getting upset? It's so automatic to move instantaneously into the victim role and justify your disturbance based upon the obvious offensiveness of the infraction. After all, who *wouldn't* be upset by such bad behavior?

It's so easy to move into "I am upset because . . ." in a flash. And then you can justify your reactions, place blame on others, and build a fortress of self-righteousness about the whole situation. Now you have a territory to protect. You stand at the ready, ever on guard, prepared at a moment's notice to sally forth with sufficient ammunition to combat any challenge to your position. Economist John Kenneth Galbraith shared this gem: "Faced with the choice between changing one's mind and proving that there is no need to do so, almost everyone gets busy on the proof."

It doesn't seem to occur to many people to question what inner part of themselves is disturbed or why what just happened is so disturbing. We recently came across a fabulous question posed by an unknown author: "Who made up these rules in the first place, and why am I following them without taking a closer look at the author?"

Now that is a fabulous query! Recall that the mind is a province of the ego and thus subject to the dualistic right/wrong process inherent in ego-based consciousness. The ego can only know what it does by observing results in the physical world and doing its best to make sense of them. It loves to figure things out. The mind is the tool the ego uses for this purpose.

To respond to this provocative question, "these rules" are taught to us all by our parents, early-childhood authority figures, and our culture in general. We derive many of them by what's modeled to us when we're small. Even overheard conversations that have nothing to do with us can result in our making errone-ous interpretations.

But Where's the Power?

But how could you take "a closer look at the author"? Try this: find a hand mirror, hold it up, and gaze into it for a few moments. You'll absolutely see the author of the rules by which you live. By "author" we don't mean the person who first fed these rules to you. Rather, you're seeing the individual who has bought into those standards and now enforces them just as severely as any dictator ever did and complies as readily as a recent military recruit.

Once you recognize the validity of this powerful realization, you can comprehend more fully Principle #13 of *Seeing Through Soul-Centered Eyes: Personal responsibility is the foundational key that opens the door to Freedom.*

Nothing prevents you from deciding for yourself what you'll choose to believe, value, support, and adhere to behaviorally. Whether you call them beliefs, rules, standards, or values, they fall into one of two categories: The first category consists of what works for you, and what you'll therefore want to maintain. The second is made up of what is limiting and no longer serving you. You'll want to look at these more closely.

Beliefs, in and of themselves, are neither positive nor negative. It's *you* who establishes your energetic charge. In *Hamlet,* Shakespeare said it this way: "[T]here is nothing either good or bad, but thinking makes it so." In such a context, the question becomes: How much of what you think—which in turn drives your behavior—is inherited from those who came before you, and how much have you consciously chosen for yourself? More important, what parts of these beliefs do you wish to preserve and what parts can change?

Remember when we asked you to imagine yourself locked in a room and tied to a chair? Well, by having you picture that scene, we established the parameters for you, and you accepted them. And remember that the way to get out was to stop imagining. This is simply another way of asking, "Are you ready to *stop imagining* and wake up from the dream of your life that's largely based upon conditioned beliefs that maintain the 'I am upset because . . .' approach?"

Regardless of how your beliefs originated, do you want to continue to live by all of them, including the ones that limit and bind you? If you do, perhaps you'd better get busy and find a way to cut the ropes on that chair, because you're locked in a room of illusion, and the hungry wolves are coming.

Taking Dominion

Over the years, we've found that the ideal opportunities for spiritual evolution also happen to be opportunities for healing our lives in general. To us it's no accident that the two are closely related. Look at the word *heal*. Perhaps the relationship would be clearer if it were written *He-all,* as in "He Is All." Within the context of Spiritual Psychology, we think of *healing* as "restoring to Essence." While we aren't aware of any research on the subject, we strongly suspect a high correlation between spiritual awareness and those who experience their lives as fulfilling. Conversely, it's a pretty safe bet that people who are prone to condemnation and violence are not the happiest of campers. In fact, we'd go so far as to say that people will tend to have less-satisfying experiences to the degree to which they're addicted to the "I am upset because . . ." approach to their lives.

The good news, as we said, is that the mental level is the easiest to work within, as it's the one to which you have the greatest access. It's also good to note that while you may have little control over what thoughts arise in your mind, you certainly have a choice about what you do with them once they're there.

What if we challenged you to simply think an uplifting thought about certain people, rather than to fall in love with them? Could you do it? Of course you could. You could choose to do so even if you considered them to be your enemies. You're not sure? Think of your worst enemy holding his or her newborn infant. See . . . it's not so hard.

We've seen a great deal of emotional-release work over the years. Our experience is that if the underlying beliefs associated with something that creates distress aren't successfully transformed, there will be no lasting, permanent healing in that person's consciousness. In other words, recalling the four-line model presented in Chapter 4, *for every negative emotional feeling, there are corresponding beliefs that support it.* Merely expressing a disturbance does little to alter the mind-set from which it flows. This may release pent-up emotions culminating in a temporary experience of catharsis, but it won't be long before the emotions begin to build again, because the underlying beliefs haven't been addressed.

It's when you release limiting ideas and reframe them into more appropriate, up-to-date points of view that you free yourself from the chronic self-victimization of "I am upset because . . ." Once the old negative view is transformed and the new, more positive one is in place, you will simply find yourself no longer experiencing reactivity, so there's no emotional buildup that takes place.

Unconsidered Beliefs Become Unconscious Habits

In Chapter 4 we pointed out that there's duality within the ego levels of the mind and emotions. Typically, people process experiences by dividing them into right or wrong. Once that duality is established, positive emotions will flow from positive beliefs. Similarly, negative thoughts are followed by negative feelings. In other words, your emotional experience aligns with your thought process.

When this process occurs frequently, the feelings tend to become anchored in the body. The more often you repeat a sequence, the more you ingrain the pattern, which then becomes a habit. This is how habitual emotional-response patterns to certain triggering situations are developed.

Further, once a habit forms, the ego conveniently generalizes, deletes, and distorts information to fit its dualistic model of reality. In other words, it categorizes similar types of experiences and tends to lose track of the underlying belief upon which an emotional reaction is actually based. When this occurs, you will literally believe that the situation itself has *caused* your response rather than the underlying belief upon which the emotional reaction is based.

Your task, then, is to find a way to "surface" the underlying beliefs that you've consciously lost track of and which have resulted in habitual emotional reactions. For example, a shy young Asian woman in class felt very apprehensive about standing up and sharing in front of the large group. Finally, after almost a year, she raised her hand and was called upon. It turned out that her fear stemmed from childhood, when she was punished repeatedly for speaking out—an impolite act in her culture. Thus, she found it more comfortable to remain in the background and withhold her opinion.

When this young woman first started at USM, she was shocked by how forthcoming many of her classmates were and fully expected them to be punished accordingly. Over time, it became obvious to her that students were receiving acknowledgment and encouragement for sharing, not punishment. Slowly, she began to shift in her consciousness, and it took the better part of a year for her to finally muster the courage and willingness to raise her hand and contribute to a discussion.

Early conditioning often fosters certain beliefs that take root within the consciousness and form an unconscious perceptual filter through which you view your experiences. It can take some work to identify and change these filters. But once the process is learned, it can be quite joyful.

Further, it's only when you dare to surface your underlying beliefs that you can discern how well they're serving you at this time in your life. If you find that some of your opinions, even those you hold deeply, no longer serve you or are outdated, you can consciously choose new ones. In this way, you have an opportunity for literally transforming your current reality. We'd like to say this again: *by changing beliefs that no longer serve you, especially deeply held beliefs, you literally transform your life, meaning that you actually alter your day-to-day experiences.* Here's our pal Emerson again: "To different minds, the same world is a hell, and a heaven." This wisdom is translated into our next principle:

Principle #17: What you believe determines your experience.

"Wait a minute," says the ego. "That's the first true thing you've said. I'm in charge of beliefs, and I can choose to believe anything I want."

The Authentic Self gently and lovingly replies, "Yes, I know you can. And you do it very well."

This reminds me of the story about three baseball umpires who are relaxing over a beer after a game, which must have taken place in my hometown of Brooklyn, New York. The first umpire says, "I calls 'em like I sees 'em."

The second says, "I calls 'em like they is."

And the third chimes in, "They ain't nothin' till I calls 'em."

It's very accurate that "there ain't nothin' goin' on in life till we calls 'em," and we "calls 'em" through what we believe to be true and valuable.

Remember the Stackers? Their job is to observe what you do and how you do it. And when you're "on course," meaning that you're learning to become more spiritually aware, they stack up different experiences than when you're "off course." The Stackers know very well that what you do is almost totally determined by what you believe. So it turns out that what you believe is essential to the quality of your everyday life experience.

The reason why this is so important is because people's lives unfold in accordance with what they believe to be true!

Since what you believe is so important, you may think that beliefs are very difficult to change. Some are! The more deeply held they are, the more difficult they can be to transform. We've seen over and over that it's relatively easy to learn the process for transforming beliefs, and some are more resistant to change than others.

"Now you're talking," says the ego. "I can change them on a dime if and when I want to."

The Authentic Self gently and lovingly replies, "Would you be willing to participate in an experiment that involves trying on some different beliefs just to see how they wear? If you don't like them, you can discard them later."

"Sure, I'm scientifically inclined," the ego boasts. "I'm open to an experiment, and as long as I'm not committing to anything, why not?"

"Excellent," replies the Authentic Self. "I admire your willingness."

And this is something we hope *you'll* experiment with right now. We've developed an easy-to-understand four-step process you can do by yourself, with a partner, or even in a group. Regardless of how many people are involved, it's a good idea to do it in a quiet place where you won't be disturbed. You might want to get out your journal, as it will also be helpful if you write down your response to each question. This can be tremendously empowering and liberating. We suggest that you allot at least 15 minutes for the process—longer if you want to work with two beliefs. We recommend working with no *more* than two, however, at any single session. Identifying and transforming just two limiting beliefs can easily change the quality of your entire life.

Soul-Centered Practice

Transforming Limiting Beliefs

1. Center your awareness in your heart and consciously look for the Loving Essence within. Bring to mind a situation that triggered a negative emotional reaction inside of you. It's best to select a recent one that's still fresh in your consciousness. What happened? How did you feel? What did you do in response?

> *Example:* I really like my job and thought I could trust one of my co-workers. I worked very hard on a project with her, and when it came time for the presentation, she took all the credit. I really felt hurt, betrayed, and devalued, but I held it in and didn't say anything. I guess she doesn't like or respect me very much, and certainly doesn't hold my contributions in high regard.

2. Assuming the premise that underlying every feeling is a belief and/or value, what were your definitions of reality associated with this situation?

Here are a couple hints:

- Ask yourself what the other person "should" have done differently.
- Or ask yourself what was "wrong" in this situation and what would be "right" according to your definitions of reality.

Example: She should have at least mentioned my contributions to the project. But she really needed to do more than that—she should have given me equal credit because I did at least as much as she did, if not more. It's just not right for her to treat me as if I don't matter. I don't want to do any more projects with such an ambitious, selfish, and inconsiderate person. If other people don't acknowledge me and my work, I must not be worthwhile.

3. Is there another perspective you *could* choose to hold about this situation that you anticipate would result in a more positive feeling? If so, what might it be?

Example: Well, if I'm willing to be totally honest, I have to admit I really don't know what her motives were, so it's possible I'm misinterpreting them. I really don't know her very well since I'm new at this job. Perhaps part of this has to do with me valuing myself and my contributions and speaking up for myself. A more accurate perspective is that my worth and value are not dependent on my work or others' acknowledgment of it.

4. If you held this new perspective, how do you suppose the situation might have turned out differently?

Example: If I simply evaluate the situation for what I can learn from it, I immediately see how I could have taken much better care of myself by talking over the presentation in advance and asking whether both our names would be appearing on it. I could have shared with her that, from my point of view, this would assist in making sure that both of our contributions would be acknowledged and respected. In fact, this is exactly what I'm going to do. I will speak with her tomorrow about recognizing my role in the project. And I know that whether or not it is acknowledged has no bearing on my worth and value.

That's all there is to it! It's that simple! And you can cycle through as many situations as you'd like for the belief you're dealing with. In each one, you'll find that a change in the belief you've held results in a change in the emotional quality of your experience. At that point, you're free to choose whether you wish to return to the original belief or stay with the new one you've just created. You may also discover that the new belief later gives way to an even more powerful one.

The goal of this process isn't for you to begin altering your entire belief structure (although you could), but rather to simply show you how easy the process can be. And, of course, if you uncover some beliefs that are in need of updating based on recent learning, by all means, feel free to revise them here and now.

As you become more conscious, the very notion of *more conscious* tends to mean that you've already changed some of your beliefs. Sometimes the changes can be easy, and sometimes they'll be more difficult. The challenge is always the same: to choose a mind-set and ensuing behaviors in accordance with the highest awareness you can muster at any given moment. Thus, the willingness to evaluate everything in service to spiritual growth is essential. For the fact of the matter is, while all views are to be respected, not all are equally valuable insofar as spiritual awakening is concerned. And different beliefs do tend to produce different results in physical-world, or Goal Line–oriented, reality.

In fact, as Dr. Hunter first told me many years ago, "You know, you don't have to be so concerned about understanding whether something is or is not so. All you really need to know is whether it works and, if it does, how to work *it*. In fact, 'what *is*' and 'what *works*' are really much better definitions of Truth than so-called factual accuracy." In addition to this understanding, we at USM have learned over the years that while a belief may be valid at one level of consciousness, it might be the very one that must be surrendered at the next level of growth.

In the next chapter, we'll identify the nature of the beliefs you hold that tend to deter you from your spiritual progression. This is essential, because once you identify them, you can more easily learn how to transform them in ways that support your spiritual evolution. This awareness is clearly expressed in *A Course in Miracles:* "Your task is not to seek for love, but merely to seek and find all of the barriers within yourself that you have built against it." And to that we would add, "and dissolve them."

Stem Sentences to Write Down and Contemplate

- If what I believe determines the quality of my life, then . . .
- One "should" that I'm aware of is based upon the belief that . . .
- I might consider changing that belief to . . .

Repeat as often as necessary.

CHAPTER EIGHT

The Ego's Back- pack: The Root of Emotional Suffering

*Add even so much as a tad of judgment to an attachment or position,
and you have amazingly strong, resilient, and resistant "issue glue."*

Imagine that it's a lovely spring day and you're enjoying a walk in the mountains. Since you're out for the day, you have a backpack with food, rain gear, and a few other essentials. You also have about 80 pounds of rocks of assorted sizes in your pack, of which you're completely unaware. Further, as you walk along, you unconsciously pick up additional rocks and add them to your burden.

You're probably wondering why in the world anyone would do such a thing, unless of course he or she was in training for the Olympics. Consider the possibility that this is exactly what *you're* doing, unbeknownst to yourself, several times every single day.

Our years of experience as educators and counselors have shown us that a minimum of 99 percent of what people feel anguish over is of their own creation. They're continually picking up rocks and adding them to their packs. We've observed how most, if not all, emotional suffering is a direct result of seeing life through ego-centered eyes that justify an "I'm upset because . . ." approach to any disturbing experience. Further, and of paramount importance, the emotional reactivity, disturbance, and pain that ensue are largely *unnecessary!*

By unnecessary, we mean that once you learn how to heal unresolved issues, you can choose whether or not to participate in life in ways that perpetuate emotional suffering. In other words, once you learn how to stop putting rocks in your pack and unload the ones that are already there, you can enjoy a life that's largely free of emotional suffering. Just to be clear, what we're calling emotional suffering refers to painful emotions such as hurt, anger, guilt, shame, resentment, loneliness, disappointment, abandonment, humiliation, and all the others we all know only too well.

So let's talk rocks! Metaphorically speaking, *rocks* are the major component of unresolved issues. And an unresolved issue is . . . anything that disturbs your peace! And *what* disturbs your peace? Well, anything you're upset about, whether it appears justified to you or not. As we discussed in Chapter 5, the main value in being aware of the "I am upset because . . ." dynamic is that it shows you precisely where the life-changing portal is that leads to the exquisite path of issue resolution. On this very path, healing, emotional freedom, and spiritual growth are found. In short, opportunities for issue resolution and spiritual evolution are both present whenever you're upset—about anything.

This leads us to another question pertaining to disturbances. We see how they function, but how are they structured? Of what are they composed? For example, you can easily see how an automobile functions. You get in, turn it on, and drive to your chosen destination. But what are the car's components and the mechanisms by which it operates? If you have such knowledge, perhaps you could see how to take it apart and put it back together again so as to enhance its functioning. Similarly, in the case of an unresolved issue, understanding the nature of the elements that compose it may provide clues and methods for resolving it in service to freeing yourself from the emotional suffering that's a by-product of chronic "I am upset because . . ."

Judging and Evaluating

To understand how an unresolved issue operates, and what its *rocks* are, let's first consider its structure. To begin, it's necessary to distinguish between two words that are often confused: *judgment* and *evaluation.* The main reason they are frequently confused is that they're often used synonymously in the English language. For example, if you were to say, "I'm a really good *judge* of wines," what you'd really be saying is that you can distinguish one wine from another, and more important, that you have the ability, knowledge, palate, and experience to judge which wine is superior based on certain criteria. In this context, the word *judge* means "evaluate."

If you look up *evaluate* in the dictionary, you'll find that it means "to determine or fix the value of." So when you *evaluate,* you're functioning as an objective, external consultant intending to examine and understand the difference between two or more possibilities, usually with the goal of producing better results. For instance, you might impartially observe a system and determine, "This is working very well, so let's leave it alone." Or you may conclude, "I'm seeing opportunities to streamline or enhance this process. Let's make a few changes, try them out, and neutrally observe the results."

You'd then experiment with the new methods and see what happens. If they prove beneficial, you might decide to implement the improvements as standard procedure. Or perhaps you concluded that the previous method was a little slower but more cost-effective, so it's better to continue using it. Or maybe you'd determine that it's functioning a little better, so your team can work to improve it even more.

The crux of the consulting, or evaluating, process is to experiment, receive feedback, *evaluate* the feedback, make adjustments, and so it goes. *Evaluating* is a neutral process. In fact, such a discipline is excellent training in developing objectivity and a consciousness of neutral observation.

The dictionary definition of *judgment* is "the process of forming an opinion or evaluation by discerning and comparing." *Discernment* is given as a synonym. When used in this way, the words *evaluation* and *judgment* are synonymous. What's essential for our purposes is the recognition that there's no emotional energy in *judging* or *evaluating* in this context. Both are objective methods of neutral observation and, if specific physical criteria can be established, are verifiable. It's very straightforward: "How's this working?" It's this process of *judging/evaluating* that's the foundation of scientific inquiry. When we *judge/evaluate* in this sense, we tend to see clearly because there's no mental bias or emotional upset feeding into the process.

The Other Side of Judgment

Now here's where the opportunity for clarification begins. The word *judgment* has another meaning. In the sense we're distinguishing here, the act of *judging* adds a mental bias (or perceptual prejudice)—as well as a negative emotional charge—to the observation. When these two elements are added, one has moved from the objectivity and neutrality of evaluation to the prejudice and emotional disturbance of a *judgmental* approach. In short, the duality of right/wrong energy has been infused into the process.

Psychologically, the act of *judging* in this sense of the word ascribes rightness or wrongness, or goodness or badness, to some person, event, or situation. This is based upon a mental bias or perceptual prejudice involving an internal rule, standard, or belief that the person doing the *judging* takes to be both true and important. Once a perceptual prejudice is built into the process, the result is an emotional upset, which then supports and reinforces the bias. Can you see how the ego has slipped into the evaluating process and turned it into the negative side of judgment?

When you see through eyes steeped in this type of judgment, you're wearing *perceptual filters,* which don't allow you to see clearly or objectively. It's sobering to consider that this type of judgmental seeing is a by-product of the way the vast majority of people on this planet have been conditioned. It's when you place these types of judgments against yourself, others, the world, and even God that they become the *rocks* you load into your backpack on a regular basis.

Judgmental thinking is the automatic by-product of looking through ego-centered eyes. What makes it toxic is the combination of negative emotional energy with righteous condemnation that stems from specific beliefs about what's right and wrong. This is where your ability to choose different beliefs—ones that serve you more fully with respect to spiritual evolution—becomes important.

Revisiting the wine example, if you're immersed in the judgmental model, it would be like saying, "This is the superior wine because *I* like it best. And because *I* like it best, it's the good wine, and all the other wines are bad. Further, I'm justifiably disturbed and upset by these bad wines' very existence and will do everything I can to destroy the vineyards that produce them."

Is this example absurd? If you think it is, instead of wine, substitute race or religion or ethnicity or culture or economic status or politics du jour, and you have a pretty accurate picture of what's reported almost every night on any news channel throughout the world.

If the world arena is too broad a context, how about the last time you got out of balance emotionally and had an "I am upset because . . ." argument with your spouse, relative, co-worker, child, or friend due to your beliefs or standards having been violated? Remember that anytime you're experiencing an emotional disturbance, you're within the ego's domain, where dualistic, judgment-based thinking is operating; and your actions will tend to be reactive rather than carefully considered. The following is a visual representation of this process.

Figure 13

JUDGING
(Seeing Through Ego-Centered Eyes)

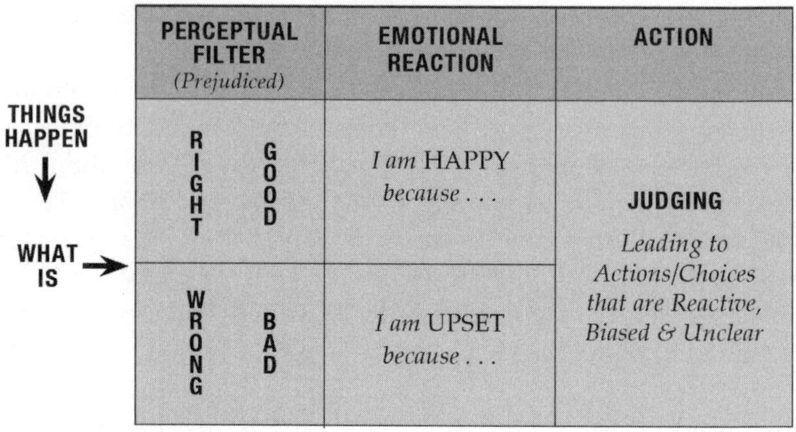

	PERCEPTUAL FILTER *(Prejudiced)*		EMOTIONAL REACTION	ACTION
THINGS HAPPEN ↓	R I G H T	G O O D	*I am* HAPPY *because . . .*	**JUDGING** *Leading to Actions/Choices that are Reactive, Biased & Unclear*
WHAT IS →	W R O N G	B A D	*I am* UPSET *because . . .*	

The way this process functions is that you begin by simply acknowledging that things happen, and this is an accurate definition of *what is*. Whatever happens *is* what is! For example, your present reality is that you're reading this page in this book. But that's not all your reality. You're also alive, a particular age and gender, a resident of a certain country, and so on. But what's happening in this moment is that you're reading this page in this book.

As you're reading, hopefully you're considering the ideas being presented. It's at this point that *what is,* the experience of reading information being processed in your mind, immediately passes through a perceptual filter, which consists of conditioned *beliefs.* Some of these *beliefs* are based on early interpretations of childhood experiences—while some are stemming from what you were taught, and some from what was modeled by others.

Functionally, perceptual filters are *judgmentally* based and have the effect of dividing personal reality into the duality of right and wrong. In other words, an experience passes through your perceptual filter, which—like a prism dividing light rays into the rainbow of colors contained within the visible spectrum—divides your experiences into good or bad. In the case of consciousness, the "prism" that does the sorting comprises your beliefs.

Your most deeply held beliefs form your personal philosophy—the way you *perceive* how things truly are or should be. No small matter are these deeply held beliefs, yet they're so firmly rooted in your psyche that they tend to operate automatically. You're often completely unaware of their presence or impact on your life.

Minds, in and of themselves, are neutral. Beliefs are a major part of their content. If you think of the mind as hardware, beliefs are the software programs that have been loaded into memory through childhood conditioning and your interpretations of early experiences.

Whose Are the "True" Beliefs?

Many people are unaware of this process. They simply assume their beliefs to be "the truth." It's rare when individuals stop to consider the possibility that their beliefs can be altered and that others may better serve them. Usually, information is received in the form of perceptions. These perceptions are then interpreted and sorted into *right* or *wrong* based upon the filter of one's beliefs. What follows is an emotional reaction congruent with the understanding the filter has imposed. And then, of course, actions are taken in the physical world consistent with the interpretation.

Naturally, you will feel justified in your actions based upon the *rightness*—or, more accurately, the *righteousness*—inherent in your personal belief system. And, of course, if your family, tribe, society, or culture agrees with the way you believe, you'll feel validated and your positions are reinforced.

Now, this way of being in the world can be relatively functional as long as what's represented in your perceptual filters is fairly benign or you live in close proximity to others who have similar beliefs. Here's an example of how perceptual filters work: If you were presented with a recipe for beef stew, you'd most likely simply decide whether or not you wanted to prepare the meal to find out if you like it. The tasting and eating would be a process of *evaluating.*

But what if you were from a culture that reveres cows as sacred or were a devout vegetarian? When you saw the recipe, you might immediately move into judgment and consider the recipe, as well as its author, very wrong. You might feel offended, experience righteous anger, notice queasiness in your stomach, or even slam the book shut . . . all of which you would consider to be very justified. You might even go to the extreme of taking the book out and burning it as a purification ritual. Can you see how this fits with the "I am upset because . . ." approach discussed in Chapter 5?

Or let's say that someone you love has recently died. If your belief system defines death before a certain age as a bad thing—a medical failure—or something that shouldn't have happened, you'll most likely feel upset about the experience. You may be very angry and even go so far as to sue the attending physician for malpractice. And it wouldn't be uncommon for you to be quite angry with God for unjustly taking your loved one in his prime. The funeral or memorial service you'd orchestrate might very well be a somber event.

In both of the preceding two examples, the right/wrong judgment model was employed, and a negative reaction ensued. *In fact, the best indicator of whether you're operating within the right/wrong model is to observe your emotional reactions to events and situations in your life.* If you have a negative emotional reaction to a situation, as you can see from Figure 13, you are engaged in the right/wrong approach with respect to that particular situation. Every time you say, "I am upset because . . ." you're seeing through ego-centered eyes.

Referring again to Figure 13, you can see that even when you enter into "I am happy because . . ." you still engage in dualistic thinking that's a by-product of the judgmental approach because you're ascribing your internal state to an outer cause. But because people don't seek assistance when they're feeling good, they rarely consider the dynamic as the same. In other words, whether you say "I am upset because . . ." or "I am happy because . . ." you're involved in the same ego-centered, dualistic way of being in the world.

To see how this works, let's look again at the example of the death of a loved one. What if your personal beliefs are such that his passing, although a significant loss for you, is a blessing, especially because he'd been quite ill and in severe physical pain, from which he's finally been released? While you may grieve your loss, you could also feel grateful that he's no longer suffering. When speaking about the experience, you may very well say, "I am grateful because . . ." You may make a generous gift to a worthy cause in his honor, or even get down on your knees and thank God for releasing him. The memorial service you plan could very well be a heartfelt celebration of his life.

Of course, we're not proposing that individuals give up their positive feelings in order to move ahead spiritually. In fact, the more people progress on their path, the more aliveness and joy they tend to experience. *The difference is, the Joy that stems from spiritual growth isn't based upon an outer cause. Rather, it emanates from within the Authentic Self, independent of outer circumstances.*

What's important for the purposes of this book is to understand that the right/wrong judgmental approach—the dualistic, ego-based approach we've been discussing—always results in unnecessary emotional suffering *when* it's based upon the "I am upset because . . ." way of life. Said another way, whenever you're engaged in the process of "I am upset because . . ." you're not functioning in a consciousness of neutral observation and *evaluation*—you're in perceptual prejudice and judgment, and you'll always experience emotional pain as you continue adding rocks to the load in your backpack. All of this is courtesy of the ego's sense of small-self importance and its addiction to seeing through the dualistic perceptual filters of *right* and *wrong*.

Accepting—the Alternative Approach

To reside in *Acceptance* is a radically different way to be in a world predisposed to judgment and "I am upset because . . ." The word *radical* often means movement away from an accepted or traditional approach. And since the traditional approach for the overwhelming majority of us is the right/wrong, "I'm upset because . . ." judgmental model, daring to break away from the familiarity and security of one's comfort zone often takes a great deal of courage.

In her book *Anatomy of the Spirit,* Caroline Myss refers to this process of getting free as emerging from "tribal culture." She says: "Our spiritual power grows when we are able to see beyond the contradictions inherent in tribal teachings and pursue a deeper level of truth." You could replace "tribal teachings" with those of family, society, or any close-knit group whose standards you take for your own. The choice is to either automatically, unconsciously subscribe to these long-held group beliefs, or do the inner work to evaluate and consciously decide for yourself what beliefs you'll choose to live by.

Figure 14

ACCEPTING
(Seeing Through Soul-Centered Eyes)

THINGS HAPPEN ↓ WHAT IS →	PERCEPTUAL FILTER *(Prejudiced)*	EMOTIONAL REACTION	ACTION
	Objectivity & Neutral Observation	*Acceptance, Compassion, Peace & Equanimity*	**OBJECTIVE EVALUATING** *Leading to Actions/Choices that are Unbiased, Neutral & Clear*

In looking at Figure 14, as with the *judgmental* model shown in Figure 13, begin with the awareness that things happen. So far, you're on solid ground. Whatever has happened *is* what is. As the event enters your field of awareness, you don't separate it into right and wrong. You simply observe what has happened and Accept it. As the wonderfully refreshing teacher and author Byron Katie says, "When I argue with reality, I lose—but only 100 percent of the time."

Can you see the immediate benefits of choosing a state of *Acceptance* and a process of *evaluation* rather than a state of *judgment* infused with emotional upset and *condemnation?*

When you *judge,* you pretend to be sure of what's spiritually correct in any particular situation. But most people can't claim the infallible knowing that comes with spiritual sight. Therefore, how can you *judge* when you recognize that you aren't consciously aware of the spiritual curriculum for any given individual in any specific situation? As Dr. Hunter once said, "You have no idea how hard the inner masters have to work to get all the appropriate people on the plane that's going to go down." The only spiritually aligned choice is to *Accept* what is and discern what, if any, action you want to take.

Within such a frame of reference, the emotion present is a deep feeling of Compassion. Why Compassion? Because to the Authentic Self, whose nature is Love, it's *the only response possible* to suffering of any kind, whether it's our own or another's. The Authentic Self is simply incapable of judging because it knows that all of life serves a spiritual purpose, regardless of whether or not it's known or understood. All we're capable of experiencing when we're centered within the Authentic Self is Love, so its outward flow extends to all life—whether it involves suffering or joy.

From within the consciousness of the Authentic Self, you Accept all the suffering and pain because you recognize that you don't know the spiritual opportunity or potential blessing existing within it. While there may be little or nothing you can do to alter what has occurred, there's one thing you can always do: choose to be with those who are suffering in a Compassionate and supportive way while they go through whatever they're dealing with. Many people aren't aware of this, but the dictionary definition of the prefix *com-* is "with." And the root of the word *passion* is the Latin *passio,* which means "suffering." So *Compassion* literally means to be with one who is suffering. We once heard spiritual teacher Ram Dass quoting his own teacher as having said that the only emotion remaining in a totally realized being is "infinite, unbearable compassion."

If you are operating from within the ego-based judgmental model, your actions will always be consistent with your right/ wrong orientation, and will thus tend to be biased, shortsighted, and self-serving. If you attempt to alleviate suffering, you'll do so out of pity for the person in pain. Your actions are actually reactions from the ego-based perspective of "What they're going through is terrible. It would be awful if I had to go through that, too. I feel so sorry for them." This approach places those who are suffering in the victim mode and demonstrates a lack of spiritual awareness; for truly, how can you know what opportunity other people's Souls are deriving from their experiences?

A Lesson in Compassion 101

The nature of Compassion was poignantly brought home to me when I began my doctoral studies in counseling psychology at New Mexico State University in Las Cruces. Think 8 A.M. statistics class! Not my favorite time or best subject, but hey, my job was to master statistics, so I became an absolute whiz at note taking. I would write copious notes in my own unique brand of shorthand and then, immediately following class, rewrite an expanded version that would be more useful later when I needed to study for an exam.

There was a gentleman in a motorized wheelchair who regularly sat next to me in class. His name was Larry, and he was a quadriplegic as a result of a trampoline accident that occurred when he was training for the Olympics. Holding on to anything with his hands was a great effort. Yet here he was, with a pen gripped in a closed fist, painstakingly scribbling notes. He could manipulate the stick controlling the speed and direction of his chair, but there was no way he could write at the speed required to get all the information down. Being a bright guy, he quickly saw that he was sitting next to Mr. Note-Taker Extraordinaire and asked if he might have copies of mine. I said yes, and gave him a copy of my detailed version following every class.

We started to get to know each other, and at one point I said, "You know something—it looks like we're becoming friends."

His response was the last thing I expected. "I don't think so."

"Why not?" I asked. Frankly, I was shocked.

"Because," he said, "you see me as a victim in this chair, and you feel sorry for me. As long as you see me like that, we could never have a true friendship because your pity would always get in the way. If you could get past that, I think we could become friends."

He was right, and I was chagrined. I was feeling pity for him and judging his condition as "terrible." Once I could admit my judgments, I could let them go. I'm glad to say that I did get past them, and we became friends who still correspond to this day.

A Vision of the High Ground

What does it look like when someone has let go of the judgmental approach to life in which most of us routinely engage? A good example was Mother Teresa, as she attended to the poorest of the poor in the slums of Calcutta. In a documentary we recently watched, she lifted a child out of the gutter and carried him toward a vehicle that would take him to one of her centers to receive care. The child was severely emaciated, encrusted with dirt and scabs, and barely alive. As she held him, she looked into his eyes and said, "What a beautiful child of God." Watching her brought tears to our eyes.

This distinction between *Acceptance-based evaluation* and *prejudice-based judgment* is vitally important since *the* single greatest challenge currently facing the human species is judgmental thinking—making stuff up and dividing everything into right or wrong. You don't have to look very far to see that the lengths people are willing to go with their rightness and wrongness include nothing short of violence, atrocities, and even war. Imagine how deeply ingrained certain negative beliefs must be for some people to be willing to kill themselves and others because of different beliefs. And of course, the most significant historical set of *apparent* differences centers around views about God: "Our way is the right way—and if you don't believe our way, you are the heretic, infidel, or blasphemer; and in the name of God, we will kill you." How ironic, since the essence of all great spiritual traditions is Loving, and the Bible even says to "love one another" (John 13:34). Humanity is dealing with a very strange distortion here.

Fortunately, it's easy to see that you do know how to function in the Acceptance-based evaluation mode, and we think we can prove it to you. If you've ever been a parent or witnessed a young child learning to walk, you know you won't see much walking at all, especially at first. Instead, you'll see numerous tentative steps and lots of falling. In this situation, it's natural to simply Accept and evaluate the child's efforts.

What you'd be highly unlikely to do is complain to your spouse that your child is doing a terrible job because she's spending most of her time falling and not walking. You wouldn't ridicule her process as filled with mistakes (since falling isn't walking), or judge her for her substandard, inferior performance.

No one would be so foolish as to do that. We all understand the process of learning to walk, so we have Compassion for the stumbling youngster, and we encourage and support her. We praise her efforts, and we comfort her when she falls.

But are we so very different from that small child? The only distinction is that rather than learning to walk, most of us are in the process of learning to Love; and what we see, especially at first, are many of what could be called *mistakes*. So often people are involved in behaviors and attitudes that appear to be anything but Loving. However, given the magnitude of what's involved in spiritual evolution, it's wise to bear in mind that learning to Love unconditionally takes much more time and is immeasurably more difficult than learning to walk. Remember the sixth principle, that *spiritual evolution (growth) is a process, not an event?* Spiritual evolution and issue resolution, including weaning oneself from the conditioned response of judgmental wrong making, takes time. We awaken relatively slowly to new ways of seeing and being.

Fortunately, Souls have little concern with time, since they're aware that the only time is *now!* While "falling" in physical reality usually results in skinned knees at most, "falling" in the realm of learning to Love is often characterized by a considerable amount of mental anguish, along with emotional pain and suffering. A bruised knee is one thing—a bruised ego is quite another. By the way, isn't it interesting that we speak of "falling" in love?

The Hike Continues

So here you are, strolling through the mountains with a backpack full of rocks. And what are these rocks? They're nothing short of all the *judgments* you've accumulated throughout your existence. It isn't fallacious psychology when you're exhorted to "judge not lest ye be judged" (Matthew 7:1). This admonition makes perfectly good psychological and spiritual sense when you realize that every time you *judge,* you add another rock to your pack and then get to lug that extra weight around until you have the wit to unload it. In other words, whenever you *judge*, you add to the size of that particular rock, and you will carry it until you let it go.

To successfully navigate this mountainous terrain requires a twofold competency. You need to learn both if you're to grow spiritually:

1. The first has to do with the attitude of *Acceptance.* As you master the practice of *Acceptance,* you learn how to go forward without picking up any more rocks.

2. The second competency is learning the skill of releasing *judgments,* misunderstandings, misinterpretations, and misidentifications. By doing so, you release the rocks you've already collected that have been weighing down your pack for God only knows how long. We'll get to this second practice in Chapter 9.

These two competencies are closely related and, as they're learned and practiced, exponentially enhance spiritual awakening. You can only go so far by mastering just one of them.

To Accept or Judge: That Is the Question

In Chapter 4, we described the domain of the Authentic Self as distinct from the ego. Its structure is one of nonduality; its essence is Love; and its resonant frequencies are Compassion, Enthusiasm, Joy, Peace, and Acceptance. From this altitude, you neutrally observe daily events from within the context of spiritual reality. You can see and Accept that life is filled with many different expressions and diverse experiences.

When seeing from this perspective, you choose not to engage in judging. Rather, you observe and Accept what is and evaluate the available choices. Sometimes a situation presents itself that demands you choose quickly which way to go. One day, as a young man back in New York, I was entering the Brooklyn-Queens Expressway, which was anything but an "expressway" by today's standards. At that time, the on-ramps were short. I often had to wait for an opening in the flow of traffic and then accelerate like mad to get going fast enough to merge. So there I was, in my brand-new Porsche, getting ready to accelerate, when my car was rear-ended. Being young and judgmental at the time, I jumped out in a pretty angry state and started walking toward the car behind me when all of a sudden the driver's door opened and out stepped a priest, collar and all. He began apologizing at once, admitting it was his fault and asking for my forgiveness. *Hmm!* What to choose—Acceptance and inner peace or judgment and righteous indignation?

It's difficult to know in advance the results or consequences of a choice. It's a given that almost everyone has the best of intentions. However, sometimes decisions result in painful ordeals or horrendous experiences. Often, unintended consequences occur as things *happen* to us.

Many people tend to call these experiences *mistakes*. If you're immersed in the right/wrong approach, you'll judge these so-called mistakes as wrong or bad and then extend and amplify the problem by judging yourself as wrong or bad for making them. You'll experience the result of this process as emotional suffering, for you're demonstrating a lack of understanding regarding the seventh principle of Spiritual Psychology: *All of life is for Learning.*

But now, from the Authentic Self vantage point, you can more consciously choose to Accept, evaluate, and gain understanding from these events. You'll no longer need to judge them as mistakes.

You'll see them as opportunities within the context of the bigger spiritual picture where they're revealed to be precisely what provided you with feedback for purposes of learning. Further, you'll now rest in the assurance that, if you don't benefit from your experiences, your personally assigned Stackers will provide you with endless additional tests of a similar nature. In fact, you can count on it.

If you learn nothing else from reading this information, we hope you will learn this: *There is no experience you've had or so-called mistake you've ever made, or will ever make, that justifies your judging yourself as bad, wrong, unworthy, a failure, defective, or any other word you would choose to use.* How do we know this? Remember the second and fourth principles: *The nature of God is Love!* and *Since we are all part of God, our nature also is Love. . . .*

From this vantage point, there's no right and wrong in the learning process. There's no blame or fault, no "I am upset because . . ." no judgment, no condemnation, and no mistakes. There are only choices and consequences within an all-encompassing spiritual context of Acceptance, Peace, Compassion, Joy, and Love. You Accept it all and always go for the learning.

If you'd like a prescription for a Grace-filled life, resolve here and now to refrain from judging anyone or anything, most of all yourself, from this day forward. Instead, set an intention to live in a state of Acceptance, which means Accepting yourself, others, the world, God, and what is. *There's no more argument with what is.* We're talking about a state of awareness characterized by non-positionality—about anything. The result is freedom from unnecessary emotional suffering. And ironically, most areas of your life will improve, often including your physical well-being, your relationships, and even your finances.

It's been said that Acceptance is the first law of Spirit, and we certainly agree. Learning to suspend judgment means learning to let go of the habit of moving into "I am upset because . . ." due to judgmentally based prejudice.

Thus, it's time to sincerely consider the next principle of *Seeing Through Soul-Centered Eyes:*

Principle #18: A life filled with Acceptance is a life devoid of unnecessary emotional suffering. It's a life filled with Love.

When you *see* clearly, you will *see* that every time you utter a judgment, you're adding another rock to the backpack you're unconsciously carrying around every minute of every day. The day you choose to begin living in Acceptance instead, you cease adding rocks to your already-heavy burden.

It's All Choices and Consequences

A short time ago, we were listening to a conversation between two of our friends, one of whom was talking about a recent frustrating situation. He was driving on the freeway when all of a sudden he was abruptly cut off by a driver, which almost resulted in a loss of control of his car. He shared how angry he'd gotten and how he'd done all he could to avoid having "road rage" and going after the offensive driver. He was obviously in *judgment* mode about this situation and asked our other friend if she'd ever had a similar experience.

She responded, "I really understand your reaction, and in fact I did have a similar encounter just the other day. After the initial shock of the near miss wore off, I started to think of what might be going on in that other driver's life. Maybe he was in the midst of an emergency, late for an important meeting, or just having a really bad day. So I took this situation as an opportunity to practice my spiritual work of Acceptance, and I blessed him. I also thanked him for making it very clear to me that what I now needed to do was slow down so that I could be absolutely certain I was nowhere near him on the road."

The above is a simple example from daily life that clearly distinguishes the judgmental and Acceptance approaches. Which of the two friends would you guess is more likely to meet the Stackers down the road?

"Okay, I get it! But how do I accept the things I usually judge and have been judging for most of my life?" you may ask.

That's an excellent question. It's exactly why we say that the second competency of letting go of judgments you've already made is absolutely essential for spiritual evolution. The process has to do with an unusual way of engaging in Forgiveness. By moving into *Acceptance,* which means discontinuing judging, you stop the process of adding more rocks to your pack.

It's by engaging in the unique process of Forgiveness (which we'll be discussing in the next chapter) that you begin taking the existing rocks out—sometimes one by one, and sometimes several at a time. And occasionally, you'll even remove a boulder. Metaphysically speaking, this process is akin to completing karma.

We're not saying that learning to live in Acceptance and Forgiveness is easy or that it can be mastered in a short period of time. The good news is that you don't have to do it all at once. It's more like releasing weight. Every time you let go of a pound—or a rock—you'll experience yourself as lighter. All you really need to focus on is being a bit more Compassionate and Accepting today than you were yesterday. In this context, it's good to remind yourself of the fifth Soul-Centered principle, one that bears repeating regularly and is a favorite: *Spiritual evolution (growth) is a process, not an event.*

Once you begin releasing judgments, you'll find that they're all that stand between a life filled with unnecessary emotional suffering and one filled with Love and Compassion. In the final two chapters, we'll go into detail about the Forgiveness process and how to effectively use it to clean out your backpack.

In the meantime, we thought you might like to hear what life is like when you've succeeded in releasing *judgments* and are living a life based in Acceptance. On December 10, 1997, Julia Butterfly Hill climbed up into a 180-foot-tall coast redwood in California, where she remained for more than two years in an attempt to prevent the destruction of the tree and the old-growth forest surrounding it. She was successful, and all the trees within a three-acre buffer zone were preserved.

Some activists are motivated strongly and passionately *against* something that's *wrong.* But Julia Butterfly Hill is different. She explained:

So often activism is based on what we are against, what we don't like, what we don't want. And yet we manifest what we focus on. And so we are manifesting yet ever more of what we don't want, what we don't like, what we want to change. So for me, activism is about a spiritual practice as a way of life. And I realized I didn't climb the tree because I was angry at the corporations and the government; I climbed the tree because when I fell in love with the redwoods, I fell in love with the world. So it is my feeling of "connection" that drives me, instead of my anger and feelings of being disconnected.

Julia is a passionate activist, and unique because her passion had ascended to a higher level. Emerson described it this way: "Life must be lived on a higher plane. We must go up to a higher platform, to which we are always invited to ascend; there the whole aspect of things changes."

Imagine what would happen in our world if people who were motivated to work for change in a positive direction understood that they don't work *for* something by working *against* its apparent opposite. If we follow Julia's example, we come to understand that progress in social, environmental, or political issues is an indirect by-product of individual spiritual progression.

A remarkable statement in *A Course in Miracles* echoes Julia Butterfly Hill: "The generation who brings peace will not be the generation who hates war but the generation who loves peace." That enlightened statement is equally true for you personally. Doesn't this make perfect sense? If you actively hate war, are you not increasing the sum total of negativity on the planet by adding your hate to that which already exists? If you are *for* peace, then you must choose to practice the *presence of peace*.

And the way to do this is to transform and heal whatever disturbance and negativity resides within. It's by performing this healing work that you take yourself out of the war you say you're against.

True spiritual progression is about *you*. It's about your individual freedom from judgment and emotional suffering and has little to do with results you achieve in this world.

Thus, we've arrived at our next principle:

Principle #19: *Your primary goal is not to change the school;*
your primary goal is to graduate.

It's important that we be clear, as this is a very important subject. We're certainly not advocating for passivity in the way you conduct your life. If you want to work for the environment, you have our support. If you want to ease the suffering of the many, we support that, too. All we're saying is that when you engage in those worthy endeavors, climb the tree in the spirit in which Julia did. Don't climb from "againstness"—climb from your Love.

Now let's go get those rocks!

Stem Sentences to Write Down and Contemplate

- One way I could be more accepting is . . .
- Another way I could be more accepting is . . .
- A judgment I would like to let go of is . . .

Repeat as often as necessary.

CHAPTER NINE

Self-Forgiveness: The Royal Road to Freedom

Unresolved issues are structures of the false self built upon sand, ready at a moment's notice to be blown away by the sweet breath of Love.

Not long ago, I was sitting quietly in meditation and asked my Soul, "Who are you?" Immediately, the answer appeared: "I am a ghost bound to a very small world." There was no judgment and no emotion in the response. Rather, it was stated neutrally and confidently.

I have contemplated this short exchange often, for its implications are great. My Soul knows why it's here. It knows it comes from a nonmaterial reality, and this physical world, which we mistakenly assume is all of existence, is but a "very small world."

So here we are—as Wordsworth put it, ". . . trailing clouds of glory do we come" to this very small world. And we are not "in entire forgetfulness." We aren't totally asleep. It's both our commission and our destiny to more fully awaken and, like the prodigal son, eventually return Home. What does leaving this very small world and returning Home look like?

I first witnessed the results of such a shift in an elderly gentleman who annually visited Dr. Hunter's Quimby Center and gave talks about his experiences. His name was Sadhu Grewal, and he was from India. When Grewal was a young man, Mahatma Gandhi would occasionally visit rural villages to hear people's concerns. A chair was usually set up in the public square, and local residents would line up for miles waiting their turn to speak with him. It often took many hours—sometimes days—before one actually spoke with Gandhi.

One year Grewal, who was a rather militant sort, decided to wait in line and give Gandhi a piece of his mind. As he waited, his energy of malcontent grew. He wanted to let this leader know all the things that were *wrong* in the government and what he *should* do to make them *right*.

There was a line drawn in the dirt about ten feet from where Gandhi sat, and people were queued up behind it to ensure a bit of privacy for him and each speaker. Finally, it was Grewal's turn. After many hours of waiting, he was agitated and impatient to speak. He rushed up to Gandhi, and the moment he looked in his eyes, Grewal experienced the power of the man's Love flood through him. Grewal simply fell to his knees sobbing—all of his anger drained out of him instantly, and in its place he was filled with the exquisite peace of Divine Love. Right then and there he committed to be a disciple of Gandhi and spend the rest of his life traveling as an emissary of Love, which was what he had been doing for more than 40 years and why he came to speak at Quimby Center. What a beautiful man.

✑

The process that Grewal experienced was the letting go of his anger, frustration, rage, and right/wrong agenda, all of which had resulted in years of emotional disturbance and suffering. He released his judgments in one glorious moment of surrender and found himself at Home in the Peace of God, where he resided for the remainder of his life.

The way we describe this process is that he passed through the portal of Forgiveness, sacrificing the judgments he had about anything and everything. Forgiveness can be experienced very deeply, and this is demonstrated at its most profound level in the surrender of Christ when he said, "Not my will but thine be done" (Luke 22:42).

While the magnitude of Grewal's process was unusual, it's the same one you go through whenever you let go of a single judgment. Every time you release a judgment, you take a rock out of your backpack and discard it. Unlike Grewal, most people awaken by releasing one rock at a time. Sometimes the change is so subtle that you may not even notice the upward shift, as it occurs below the threshold of awareness. For the majority of individuals, a gradual awakening is a good thing, since the alternative can be rather shocking to the nervous system—not to mention the ego. Nevertheless, when you add the weight of one released rock to that of another and that of yet another, it's not long before the aggregate lightening adds up to a transformed consciousness and a changed life.

The acclaimed novelist Henry Miller articulated a beautiful awareness of the letting-go process when he wrote: "I know what the great cure is: it is to give up, to relinquish, to surrender, so that our little hearts may beat in unison with the great heart of the world."

What might Miller have meant? What is the process of surrendering, and how can you work it? How does one move into and through the portal of Forgiveness? How can you go Home and reside in the Unconditional Love, Peace, and Joy of your True Nature? For us, these are life's most important questions.

Let's begin by returning once again to the second and fourth principles of Spiritual Psychology: *The nature of God is Love!* and *Since we are all part of God, our nature also is Love. . . .*

Assuming that you're willing to consider these principles, the question immediately arises regarding how the ego and its role in the affairs of humankind and physical-world reality relate to each other.

The Journey of Surrender

In Figure 15, you can see the duality of the ego's reactions to events in the "very small world" of physical reality. As we've explained earlier, when things go the way you believe they should, you deem them *right* or *good* and have a positive emotional reaction. You then make choices and behave in harmony with that conditioned pattern. When things aren't as you think they should be, you proclaim them *wrong* or *bad*. You then enter into the judgmental model of "I am upset because . . ." that's laced with negative emotional reactions, unclear choices, and imbalanced behavior.

Figure 15

THE EGO'S PERCEPTUAL
CONTEXT OF DUALITY

NEGATIVE PICTURE	(DUALITY/EGO LEVELS)	POSITIVE PICTURE
The way things are in the world that I don't like (Wrong • Bad)		*The way I think things should be in the world (Right • Good)*

Regardless of whether the positive or negative side of the duality is referenced, you're still operating within the framework of duality. Currently, this way of perceiving and behaving in the world is how the vast majority of people go through life. And since negative beliefs far outweigh positive ones, most people struggle through life, unconsciously walking the painful path of judgment and emotional suffering.

But that's not the whole picture. What happens when the dimension of spiritual reality and spiritual purpose is added into the picture? What are the results when you shift from traditional psychology to Spiritual Psychology?

Figure 16

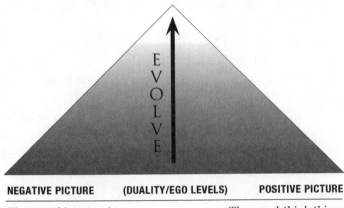

HIGHER SPIRITUAL CONTEXT =
SEEING & ACCEPTING WHAT IS = LOVE
(Home of the Authentic Self)

NEGATIVE PICTURE	(DUALITY/EGO LEVELS)	POSITIVE PICTURE
The way things are in the world that I don't like (Wrong • Bad)		*The way I think things should be in the world* (Right • Good)

Waking up spiritually means becoming more and more aware that, in addition to the horizontal dimension of physical-world reality, there's an enormous vertical dimension of spiritual reality that you're also traveling along. It's this upward journey that's the Soul's Learning Line and everyone's purpose in coming to the Earth School.

In this book, we've used the triangle to depict this upward movement, since our experience indicates that as things ascend, they converge. Once you begin to lift vertically, you will find yourself rising through successive levels of duality, each having slightly less energetic pull on you. Said another way, as you move upward through any set of perspectives in opposition, you become aware that the pull of the polarities lessens, and their effect also weakens as you ascend. This quality of upward shift is present every time you let go of a single judgment.

As this process continues, you find yourself becoming more accepting and peaceful. Eventually, you will reach a point where apparent dualities dissolve, as well as the tension that existed between them. Here you reside in a state of Acceptance. You're in Peace! It's the altitude of spiritual awareness that changes your perspective, which in turn transforms everything and alters the way you see the world.

When *Seeing Through Soul-Centered Eyes,* you become aware that arguing one set of beliefs against another, which is the substance of all ego-based conflict, is like pitting chocolate against vanilla. Perhaps this is what Albert Einstein meant when he said, "Problems cannot be solved by the same level of thinking that created them."

If we may be allowed to interpret Einstein, the only real possible solution is to dissolve the apparent dualities of the perceived conflict by placing them into a higher context. Thus, as you move from ego-centered reality to Soul-Centered reality, all opposing points of view slowly disappear, and what eventually emerges is a single vantage point from which everyone is in alignment with the highest good of all concerned. Said another way, as you ascend, conflict dissipates and Peace is present. You experience the all-encompassing Love that's the substratum of all existence and which lies beneath all apparent dualities.

Poet and philosopher Eli Siegel expressed this awareness in his well-known proposition: "All beauty is a making one of opposites, and the making one of opposites is what we are going after in ourselves."

You need only look at the events of the day to see this dynamic at play. For example, two nations might stop fighting one another if they realized that they could each have more of what they truly wanted by peacefully cooperating. That neither can seem to see the wisdom of such an approach isn't so much a statement about intention or inherent goodness as it is a commentary on evolution in the consciousness of those involved.

Similarly, a small child's ignorance of the dangers of running into the street is less a statement about his intelligence as it is about his state of development. He simply hasn't yet learned about, or hasn't yet evolved to the point that he comprehends, the inherent danger of rapidly moving vehicles. At some stage, he'll learn about speeding cars, and then the danger will become obvious and his behavior will no longer need to be monitored.

There will be a time when we as a species will arrive at a level of evolution such that it will be obvious and accepted that much more is to be gained by working together than by fighting. Perhaps that time is now! As our scientist friend Dan Fry used to say, "From a statistical point of view, there can be no doubt that there is intelligent life on other planets elsewhere in the universe, which gives me great hope that someday there may be intelligent life on this one, too." We knew Dan well enough to know that what he was talking about when he used the word *intelligent* was probably better expressed with the word *evolved*. And isn't it fascinating that *love* spelled backward is the root of the word *evolution?*

Ego—What's the Point?

So now that you have a sense of the more encompassing context of spiritual reality, you may be asking yourself what students at USM often ask: *Why do I even have an ego? Why do I have an aspect of my consciousness that creates so much suffering? Aside from stuffing my backpack full of rocks, what is its role?*

Although egos *seem* to be in opposition to your awakening into the awareness of who you are, at your core, like everything else, egos are serving a spiritual purpose. For how else could you emerge from your sleep if you weren't physically present in your self-created *very small world?* However, while your small-self personality (ego) does exist within the larger context of Love (God is Love), it can only be aware of Love as a concept or feeling. What it *doesn't* appear to be aware of is the experience of Love as a continual state of revelation or being such as that experienced by Sadhu Grewal.

And as hard as it might be for our egos to admit, hardly any of us really knows our own spiritual curriculum—much less the spiritual curriculum of others. We see what we perceive as pain and suffering, and we make all sorts of assumptions and interpretations about what that means. The possibility doesn't seem to dawn on us that maybe, just maybe, we're all really doing the best we know how given our current levels of spiritual development. Might it even be that everything is moving forward on an upward path of spiritual evolution (see Figure 16) regardless of how it appears to us in physical-world reality? From this higher perspective, everything is simply opening up into its more evolved state, much like the bud opens into the fullness of the rose.

Such a view would mean that even when you enter into judgment, you're doing the best you know how to do at that time. However, while all beliefs are to be respected—even those underlying judgments—not all of them are equally valuable insofar as spiritual awakening is concerned, nor are they equally useful for living a fulfilling life. Beliefs resulting in judgment merely encourage, support, and maintain the illusion of victimhood and the emotional suffering that follows.

We cannot emphasize enough the importance of this awareness, especially in the context of life on Earth, as it exists today. *While all beliefs and points of view are to be respected, they vary greatly as far as the consequences of believing them are concerned. Some beliefs support people in moving higher in consciousness, into higher states of Love; while others—particularly those containing misunderstanding and judgment—encourage, support, and perpetuate physical and emotional suffering.*

From the higher perspective, even when you clearly see that certain beliefs result in emotional suffering, you still choose to honor everyone's unique spiritual curriculum. "We must be willing," as we always say at USM, "to give people the dignity of their process"—to give them the space to learn through their own experiences. We love the way this attitude was expressed by the Findhorn Community in *The Findhorn Garden:* "Flowers unfold slowly and gently, bit by bit in the sunshine, and a soul, too, must never be punished or driven but unfolds in its own perfect timing to reveal its true wonder and beauty."

To be true to your Authentic Self means that you choose to reside in the consciousness of Acceptance. From that altitude, you allow people the dignity of their process, knowing full well that some of their behaviors, based upon certain beliefs, will have consequences that will eventually result in Stacker involvement.

What many of us don't realize is that with each judgment we condemn *ourselves* to more emotional suffering, simply because we're choosing to hang out in judgment. Then the Stackers (with great compassion) say, "Stack up ten more experiences." From the perspective of spiritual awakening, it's necessary for them to continue stacking until we catch on that waking up is the order of the day and that we have the opportunity to choose our attitude even in the most difficult of circumstances. This opportunity is vital to our spiritual evolution, for as we say in the 16th principle: *How you relate to an issue is the issue, and how you relate to yourself while you go through an issue is the issue.*

♋♋

Let's be clear! As long as you are primarily ego referenced, your belief system emanates from the perspective that experiences in life are to be judged on the basis of what happens in physical-world reality. What we're talking about is the difference between an ego-referenced belief system and life within the context of the Authentic Self. Said another way, it's the difference between the fool's gold of the ego's promise versus the true gold of waking up into spiritual reality and *Seeing Through Soul-Centered Eyes.*

Forgiving . . . Without Being Right or Wrong

If we had to encapsulate Spiritual Psychology into one simple but wonderful conclusion, it would be that our purpose for being alive is fulfilled by moving more and more deeply into our spiritual hearts and experiencing the presence of Love. If Spirit is the Essence, Love is its language, and it is Love that is the healing agent in consciousness. It is Love that dispels judgment and heals the painful illusion of separation. And it is Love that allows us to awaken. At this point, we're ready for a most powerful principle:

Principle #20: *Healing is the application of Loving to the places inside that hurt.*

Healing is merely the experience of letting go, which is another way of saying *Forgiveness*. It's a method for resolving unresolved issues—any and all of them! Even in the domain of the physical body, what is healing if not the letting go of disease? And is that not a Loving action?

The notion of Forgiveness is certainly not new. However, the word *forgiveness,* like any other, can be used in more than one way. For this reason, it's important to distinguish its precise meaning within the context of Spiritual Psychology so that you may be successful in releasing yourself from judgment and the associated emotional suffering. Most often, when someone says, "I forgive," what they mean is: "Even though what you did was wrong, I'm willing to forgive you for doing it." For example, someone might say, "All right, I forgive you for the terrible way you treated me," or "I forgive you for hurting my feelings." You get the picture.

This type of forgiving is important, as it's a valid way of moving in the direction of letting go. It's a way of challenging the ego to release grudges and resentments, which it feels justified in holding on to. When entered into with sincerity, this is a beautiful and uplifting experience for the forgiver.

But do you notice anything interesting in the previous two forgiveness statements? It's a subtle yet extremely important distinction. Do you notice that they both contain the duality of right and wrong? Can you see the "I am upset because . . ." basis for what's being forgiven? In these examples, while the intention to forgive is laudable, the actual process of forgiving is being done from the ego's perspective. When this type of forgiveness is practiced, usually what the person has actually done is enter into a more subtle level of the right/wrong model. However, a judgment that what the other person did was wrong is still being held on to. It's the ego that's essentially saying, "How you treated me was awful, but I'm a big enough person that I can forgive you for it." So while this type of forgiveness is going in a healthy direction, it will do little to dissolve the rocks in one's backpack, as it doesn't address the actual judgment that underlies the person's inner disturbance.

The Forgiveness that we're bringing forward here doesn't emanate from the ego's positional point of view, but rather from the heart of the Authentic Self. Within this context, true Forgiveness is accomplished by surrendering judgments and thus transcending the right/wrong levels of the mind and emotions. It's a process of entering into the Authentic Self—the consciousness of Unconditional Loving. "Hmm!" you may be saying. "How can I do that?"

Let's begin by asking a spiritually referenced question: How can you *absolutely* know what "wrong" means in any given situation?

Answer: You can't. But when you judge, you act as if you know the spiritual purpose with respect to whatever you're judging. You're claiming to know that whatever happened (that you don't like) should not have happened the way it did. In so doing, you pretend to know God's Will, at least regarding this particular situation.

When you behave in accordance with the ego's assumption of God's Will, without realizing it you're actually making choices that are out of alignment with God's Essence, which is Infinite, Unconditional Love. When you act in this way, you will receive feedback designed to let you know that you're not in harmony with Unconditional Love. The ego experiences pain and emotional suffering, but when you're *Seeing Through Soul-Centered Eyes,* you recognize that these are simply feedback responses letting you know you're missing the mark and not embracing these signs as opportunities for issue resolution and awakening.

Because you don't know spiritual purpose absolutely, isn't it obvious that you're making up these rules based mostly on nothing other than what your ego has come to believe is *the way life should be?*

So when you forgive anyone, including yourself, for doing things that you define as *bad* or *wrong,* you run the risk of subtly reinforcing the judgment you've initiated.

What, then, *can* you forgive? How can you experience the healing balm of Authentic Self-Centered Forgiveness?

It's time to hold on tight. Here we go!

Soul-Centered Self-Forgiveness

When seeing through the Soul-Centered Eyes of the Authentic Self, where Unconditional Loving is reality, the only things you can truly forgive (let go of) are the judgments that you've initiated against anything or anyone, including yourself. It's your own judgments stemming from unresolved issues that result in emotional suffering. *You* are the one who experiences the pain of separation whenever you judge. If the Essence of God is continual and ongoing Love, it's not from God that you need to seek Forgiveness. It's from yourself!

Spirit's own Unconditional Love provides endless opportunities to bring yourself back into alignment with Infinite Love. Everyone is given innumerable chances to learn from them. If this weren't so, then the instant you uttered the first judgment you'd be condemned for eternity. There would be no way to return Home.

You might ask, "Why would we do that to ourselves?" What a fabulous question. The answer is, we wouldn't if we really knew what we were doing. *It's our ignorance, our lack of awareness, which results in emotional suffering.* The good news is that as soon as you're ready, you can learn how to let go of judgments. You *can* release them, just as you'd discard a five-pound rock you've been carrying around.

But what about all the admonitions you grew up with? What about getting down on your knees and asking God for forgiveness? When you do that, the Divine, out of Its Infinite Love, looks down upon you with great Compassion and answers your prayer. However, the answer may not be the one you're praying for, but rather one that provides an opportunity for you to experience the cessation of your perceived separation. If you listen carefully, you might hear this:

It is not for Me to forgive you for your judgments, as I am not the one who placed them out into eternity. All I do is Love you, for that is My nature; and because of that, My Grace is always available for you. And since Love is all I know, I am not judging you. I will never make you wrong, and there is never anything you can think or do for which I will judge you. And because I Love you, might I offer you some counsel? Since you are the one who issues judgments, you are the one who is best equipped to dissolve them. You do this by compassionately forgiving yourself for pretending to know My Will and judging according to your limited understanding.

As soon as you forgive your judgments, My Grace enfolds you and you are truly forgiven. And I Love you enough to allow you to evolve into this awareness of your Self through freedom of choice. Each choice bears a consequence. Eventually, you will learn to make choices that result in Loving rather than suffering. By so doing, you will come to realize your full potential and truly become one with Me. And further, you have an infinite amount of time for your learning process.

Personally, we take this as extremely good news, since it places the rate of one's spiritual evolution squarely in one's own hands. Once you're ready to relinquish the victim role of "I am upset because . . ." and accept 100 percent responsibility for what you create, you set yourself up for considerably more rapid progress. In the context of spiritual reality, it's all a natural process of choices and consequences. If you choose to judge, you receive the consequences (feedback) of emotional suffering, and in extreme cases this includes the pain and anguish of perceived separation from God. If you choose to forgive, the consequence is that the door to Love opens wide and your whole life transforms.

And it's the job of the Stackers to provide a continual stream of situations (opportunities) to which you will choose your responses. The Stackers are aware that you don't respond in a vacuum. And they know that you act in accordance with what you believe to be true, valuable, and important. Thus, *how* you behave is a valid indicator of *what* you believe. Similarly, the feedback you receive from your actions is a valid indicator of how well those beliefs are working for you. In the words of William James, "Each of us literally *chooses,* by his way of attending to things, what sort of a universe he shall appear to himself to inhabit."

It's this opportunity of releasing the judgments you—yourself, in your ignorance—have initiated that forms the basis, power, and Grace for what we refer to as Compassionate Self-Forgiveness. Once you recognize that you're simply learning to be more Loving (since being more Loving is being more Godlike), you've arrived at the next principle:

Principle #21: *Loving, Healing, and Evolving are all the same process.*

It's highly likely that readers of a book such as this would want to be in the Loving, Healing, and Evolving business. The good news is that you get to do exactly that to the degree that you're willing to retire from the judging business. As we've said, once you quit judging, you enter the world of Acceptance, where you find significantly decreasing amounts of emotional suffering, which has now been replaced with greater Joy, Peace, Compassion, and Love.

Leaving the Rocks Behind

All right! Now you know how to stop adding more rocks to your pack. Let's get to the business of dissolving the ones that have already been collected. And perhaps, like Sadhu Grewal, you may drop a significant portion of the entire pack all at once.

As it turns out, the rocks you want to set down stem from nothing more than an accumulation of a particular variety of beliefs—those having to do with thoughts of blame and condemnation that we refer to as judgment. Judgment is the major obstacle to freedom from unnecessary emotional suffering. For most people, it's what stands in the way of the Peace and Joy for which they so deeply yearn. The process of entering into judgment is the instrument the ego uses to perpetuate the myth that humans have somehow separated themselves from the Absolute, as if that were possible.

Until you recognize this, you are stuck and will continue to suffer emotionally.

Compassionate Self-Forgiveness is the process that dissolves judgments and brings a healing balm of Compassion to the places inside where there's emotional pain. Without this process, freedom from emotional suffering would be impossible. You'd exist eternally in a self-created hell, and feel as if you were cast out of the Garden of Eden, with no chance to return. *Compassionate Self-Forgiveness* is your return ticket and the simplest and most effective way we know of to return Home. It's by the healing act of forgiving yourself for judging that you are liberated.

Compassionate Self-Forgiveness is the mechanism by which you dissolve the rocks you've erroneously placed in your backpack out of ignorance. You simply weren't aware of what you were doing.

What happens when you fail to forgive—either because of an unwillingness to get off your position or a lack of awareness that such a healing action is possible, much less readily available? Or perhaps you simply don't know how.

We can't begin to count how many family situations we've worked with that involve these negative dynamics. One in particular that stands out had to do with a young man named Robert who had two brothers. The three siblings were in a family business in which their father, who founded the business, was still active, although he was aging and slowly relinquishing control.

The three sons were competing for their dad's favor and the position as the next head of the company. As time went on, Robert rose to the top and was named managing director. Both of his brothers reacted to his promotion by leaving the business. One left cordially enough, but the other did so with considerable animosity. He felt betrayed by his father because he wasn't chosen for the top job. This brother had two lovely children who were the light of their grandparents' eyes. However, when he left the business, although he continued to live in the same city, his judgment and subsequent resentment surrounding his dad's decision led him to close and harden his heart. In fact, he went so far as to refuse to allow his parents to see their grandchildren.

Sad to say, this story didn't have a happy ending. The elderly parents didn't live much longer and never again experienced the joy of spending time with their grandchildren, nor did the kids have the benefit of being with their loving grandma and grandpa—all because of judgment, hurt feelings, and an unwillingness to get off a position.

Judgment always results in hurt feelings, separation, withholding, and justification of anger and resentment. The bottom line—judgment will always result in emotional suffering.

So how do you know if and when you're in judgment? There's an easy way to tell: Apply the "I am upset because . . ." test. If you're upset, meaning your peace has been disturbed—about anything—you'll invariably find judgment somewhere in your thought process and suffering in your emotions.

Another way to tell is by asking yourself, "Am I making someone or something wrong?" or "Do I have hurt feelings about a rule or standard that has been violated?" If your answer is yes, there's judgment present. The more disturbed you are, the more you'll feel and believe that your position is *right* and that the opposing one is *wrong*.

Some people are so cemented in their beliefs that they're not open to any conversation where the validity or consequences of their views can be explored. Further, these individuals will often tell you that strict adherence to their beliefs is a testament to the strength of their character, since they won't be swayed by any evidence or argument to the contrary. This brings to mind the movie *Zorba the Greek,* which Mary and I recently had the pleasure of rewatching. When Zorba said something to the effect that you can knock all day long on the door of a deaf man and he will not hear you, we knew exactly what he meant.

It's helpful to remember that while you don't have control over what happens in your life, you do have choices regarding your attitude and how you respond. Exercising the choice to engage in Compassionate Self-Forgiveness is surely a bold and daring step requiring strength of heart.

Soul-Centered Practice

Compassionate Self-Forgiveness

If you're ready to move ahead, we've developed a comprehensive nine-step process similar to the four-step one we did in Chapter 7. In the *Transforming Limiting Beliefs* process, you had the experience of becoming more flexible in your consciousness, and you saw how to change beliefs if and when you so choose.

In the *Compassionate Self-Forgiveness* process, you'll work with releasing judgments associated with specific negative beliefs that result in emotional suffering. You'll actually have an opportunity for healing at least one of them, perhaps for the last time.

As with the previous process, this can be done alone, with a partner, or even in a group. If you're doing the process alone, it's beneficial to find a quiet place where you won't be disturbed. You may want to light a candle to establish a sacred space, and you can play some soft instrumental music in the background. It's good to allow a minimum of 30 minutes to go through this process completely. It's also another good opportunity for using your journal. The following example shows how you can do this process by yourself, and you'll probably find it helpful to write out a response to each of the nine steps:

1. Center your awareness in your heart and consciously look for the Loving Essence within. Bring to mind a recent situation that triggered a negative emotional reaction inside of you. What happened? How did you feel? What did you do in response?

   Example: My husband and I were having a disagreement. I got really upset because he raised his voice. I felt hurt and reacted with anger.

2. Give your feelings a voice. Let the hurt or angry part inside speak freely, and write down what it says. Don't censor your expression, and don't be concerned with grammar or spelling. Allow the "I am upset because . . ." voice to speak freely.

Example: How can you talk to me like that after all I do for you? What's wrong with you? You're such a jerk. Why can't you understand how I feel? You never listen, and I'm getting sick and tired of all of your arrogance and insensitivity. You don't care about me at all. I'm so stupid for putting up with you, and I feel so fed up.

3. Move into a place of accepting yourself, your feelings, and the situation as a God-given opportunity that's present for your learning and growth.

Example: All right, I know that I'm really upset, and I know that this disturbance is triggering "I am upset because . . ." inside of me. I accept that I'm in this situation, which is presenting me with opportunities on the Learning Line, and I recognize that I can use them for healing.

4. Take 100 percent responsibility for your emotional reaction as a way of reclaiming dominion inside yourself and over the situation.

Example: I know this emotional upset is occurring inside of me and is based upon beliefs and judgments for which I'm responsible. I also know that this is an opportunity to identify the judgments and release them. It's my intention to heal whatever is disturbing my peace.

5. List any judgments against others and yourself that you perceive are present. They're usually easily identified from Step 2. They're the condemning, or "wrong-making," statements.

Examples:
- My husband is wrong!
- He's a jerk!
- He doesn't listen to me!
- He doesn't care about me!
- I'm stupid for staying with him!

6. Engage in Compassionate Self-Forgiveness for your judgments.

Examples:

- I forgive myself for judging my husband as wrong.
- I forgive myself for judging him as a jerk.
- I forgive myself for judging him as not listening.
- I forgive myself for judging him as an uncaring person.
- I forgive myself for judging myself as stupid for staying in this marriage.

7. When you're finished, move into your Authentic Self, a place of Self-Acceptance and Self-Compassion, as best you know how. Ask yourself what the Truth is about this situation.

Example: The truth is that he's entitled to his opinion. Really, he's a good man, and I'm grateful to be with him. I know he's doing his best to hear me, and sometimes we just don't see "I" to "I." In my heart, I know he really cares, and I'm wise enough to be releasing these judgments. Beneath it all, I love him very much.

Note: It's common when doing this quality of work that memories of older hurts and judgments of a similar nature may emerge. This is a positive indicator that deeper, more ingrained judgments can also be released.

Example: I realize that I've been in this exact situation in previous relationships. What is it inside me that draws this sort of situation to me? Oh, I see. I don't think I'm worthy of a truly loving relationship. I forgive myself for judging myself as unworthy of loving relationships. The truth is that I'm a beautiful, caring person who has a lot of Love to share. I *am* worthy of a heartfelt, loving relationship.

8. Once the negative energy has lifted and you're back in balance, look for creative solutions to the triggering situation for the highest good of all concerned. They'll usually be right there. Effective outer action follows successful inner action.

Example: I see that when my husband approaches me with irritation and anger, I can gently let him know that I would appreciate his talking to me in a kinder way. In fact, I'm going to write him a loving letter and share this with him. And I know it's a good thing for me to let him know more often how much I love and appreciate him and all he does for me. I think I'll start my letter with that message.

9. Acknowledge and appreciate yourself for your willingness to learn how to work with your disturbance as an opportunity for growth and healing.

Example: I appreciate myself for my willingness to use this opportunity to move into my own Acceptance and Compassion for both my husband and me. And on a very deep level, I'm grateful to Spirit for presenting me with an opportunity for learning how to heal the unresolved issues residing in my consciousness.

Note: The way we phrase Compassionate Self-Forgiveness statements is very important. In the example in Step 6, we use the wording, "I forgive myself for judging my husband as a jerk." This is a clear statement that "I'm forgiving *myself* for the judgment I've placed upon him pertaining to a quality that I've attributed to him."

In the heat of the situation, however, it might be tempting to say, "I forgive myself for judging my husband *for being* a jerk" or "I forgive my husband *for being* a jerk." In both of these examples, the judgment of "jerkness" is actually being affirmed, thus no forgiveness is taking place. You may need to read this paragraph a few times to see what we mean.

ᴄᴣᴏ ᴄᴣᴏ

The <u>*Compassionate Self-Forgiveness*</u> *process is the most powerful healing tool we know. We've seen it used effectively thousands of times and change countless lives.*

Sometimes people will ask what to do if they complete the process and don't feel the shift into forgiveness. This is an excellent question. Engaging in the protocol as written does not automatically assure that you are, in fact, engaging in *Compassionate Self-Forgiveness*. It's possible that you're going through the steps of the process but aren't actually engaging in the process. A clear understanding of why you're attempting it in the first place can be helpful, as it will infuse your intention and move you into the place of Self-Acceptance and Self-Compassion.

Over the years, we've discovered several keys that tend to facilitate the inner movement required for Self-Forgiveness to achieve completion. Do one, two, three, or all four of these immediately prior to Step 6:

- Think of a child you love. Allow your heart to open. From this place, go ahead and move into *Compassionate Self-Forgiveness*.

- Think of the person you love the most. Allow your heart to open. From this place, go ahead and move into *Compassionate Self-Forgiveness*.

- Think of someone who represents the highest level of Loving spiritual awareness. From this place, go ahead and move into *Compassionate Self-Forgiveness*.

- Place your right hand on your heart and allow your heart to open. From this place, go ahead and move into *Compassionate Self-Forgiveness*.

When you do the process with intention, in essence you're saying:

> I'm tired of the pain and suffering and disturbance of my own reactivity that my judgments perpetuate. I've been having the same upsetting experience over and over, and I want to be free of this pattern. My intention is to let go of my judgments and move into greater equanimity and Loving—to truly experience *Compassionate Self-Forgiveness*. I realize that by judging, I'm only condemning myself, since all I'm really doing is reinforcing my unresolved issues and digging myself deeper into the field of negativity. Right here and now, I'm letting go of my judgment that _____, by forgiving myself for having made this judgment in the first place.

When your intention is clear and you enter into *Compassionate Self-Forgiveness,* you may have one of several experiences that we've observed many times over the course of doing this work: People have reported unmistakable experiences of "being washed clean," "being flooded with love," "shaking," or "electricity running through my body," for example. This is usually followed by a profound sense of calm, well-being, and clarity. Most often, it's a feeling of something releasing, like a burden being lifted off your shoulders, followed by a sense of inner Peace. It's a beautiful experience.

"The Light Went Inside, and Stayed"

Here's how one USM student recently shared the process with her classmates:

> I've recently gone through the most painful experience of my life, which revealed a tremendous amount of shame I've been carrying with me since childhood.
>
> I was raised in a small rural town, and I was an illegitimate child, the product of an affair my mother was having. Everyone in the town knew all about it and made fun of me. I grew up feeling very unworthy, and since my mother was an atheist, I never learned how to turn to God for assistance.
>
> So when the shame began surfacing, I cried and cried. And then one of my USM classmates said to me, "You are not the circumstances of your birth." Her saying this somehow initiated a releasing process inside me, and I forgave myself for all the judgments I'd placed on myself as an unworthy person and for misidentifying who I am as the circumstances of my birth. I felt such freedom, and the pain was gone.
>
> So then I thought I'd do an inner process with myself at the age I was when I went through this experience. I was telling my inner child that she wasn't the circumstances of her birth, when all of a sudden she started going dark—like

mud. Then the mud cracked and broke away, and she began radiating this incredible Light. She wasn't the shape of a little girl anymore. She became a Being of Light that was emanating Love. She was an angel. She told me that she'd been waiting for me to be able to see her, and she began saying the most beautiful things to me. Then she asked, "Can I hold you?" And she went to hold me and said, "It's not close enough. I need to get inside you." And she's gone inside me, and I'm still shaking and pulsing from her being inside me. And you know what? I really don't care what anyone thinks of me anymore. I just feel absolutely complete. With that Light shining inside me, I know I'm truly a blessed child of God.

Consider the extraordinary similarity between this student's experience and what poet W. B. Yeats penned many years ago:

> *I am content to follow to its source*
> *Every event in action or in thought;*
> *Measure the lot; forgive myself the lot!*
> *When such as I cast out remorse*
> *So great a sweetness flows into the breast*
> *We must laugh and we must sing,*
> *We are blest by everything,*
> *Everything we look upon is blest.*

If there's any "againstness," positionality, or righteousness (all indicators that judgment is still present), your forgiveness won't go to completion, and you'll experience only a minor shift. However, this isn't necessarily bad news, for simply engaging in the *Compassionate Self-Forgiveness* process sets your intention in much the same way as does saying an affirmation. Each time you go through the nine steps, you're reinforcing your objective. As you become more sincere in your willingness to let go of judgments, your purpose strengthens until you at last come to that glorious day when you truly experience the process . . . and *Compassionate Self-Forgiveness* washes through your consciousness.

On that blessed day, your past awareness of reality will shift, and you'll know who you are. You'll stand in awe, astonished to discover that you're indeed a Divine Being having a human experience. Further, you'll discover that through it all, your Soul has been guiding your action according to its purpose. It has always been that way, and it always will.

And then you'll know why it is that Dominican theologian, preacher, and mystic Meister Eckehart would say, "If the only prayer you ever say in your whole life is 'thank you,' that would suffice."

Recently, Mary had a beautiful dream within which she and I were facilitating a class having to do with *Self-Forgiveness*. Then the scene shifted, and we were overlooking a field extending beyond where the eye could see. It was completely filled with exquisitely beautiful white irises. As she was weeping tears of joy over the magnitude and magnificence of what she was seeing, a voice spoke to her and said, "There is an iris for every act of *Compassionate Self-Forgiveness*."

Stem Sentences to Write Down and Contemplate

- I forgive myself for judging _____ as
  _____. The truth is . . .

- I forgive myself for judging myself as _____.
  The truth is _____ . . .

- I forgive myself for buying into the belief that _____
  _____. The truth is . . .

Repeat as often as necessary.

CHAPTER TEN

Self-Forgiveness in Context: The Big Picture

We're not here to please God. We're here to realize that we are *God, meaning that we're a part of God. In the moment of that revelation, we find our true freedom.*

A professor challenged his students with the following questions: "Does evil exist? Did God create evil? Did God create everything that exists?"

A student bravely replied, "Yes, He did!"

"God created everything?" the professor asked.

"Yes, sir," the student answered.

The professor smiled. "If God created everything, then God created evil. Since evil exists, and according to the principle that our work defines who we are, then God is evil."

The student became quiet and didn't offer a response. The professor, quite pleased with himself, boasted to the class that he had proven once more that religious faith was a myth.

Another student raised his hand and said, "Can I ask you a question, Professor?"

"Of course," the man replied.

The student stood up and asked, "Does cold exist?"

"What kind of question is this? Of course it exists. Have you never been cold?"

The other students snickered at their peer's question.

The young man replied, "In fact, sir, cold does not exist. According to the laws of physics, what we consider cold is, in reality, the absence of heat. Every body or object is susceptible to study when it has or transmits energy, and heat is what makes a body or matter have or transmit energy. Absolute zero, which is approximately −460 degrees Fahrenheit, is the total absence of heat; all matter becomes inert and incapable of reaction at that temperature. Cold does not exist. We have created this word to describe how we feel when we have no heat." The student paused before continuing, "What about darkness? Does it exist?"

"Of course it does," the professor retorted, somewhat impatiently.

The student countered, "Sir, darkness does not exist either. Darkness is in reality the absence of light. Light you can study, but not darkness. In fact, while you can use Newton's prism to break white light into many colors and study the various wavelengths of each one, you cannot measure darkness. A simple ray of light can break into a world of darkness and illuminate it. How can you know how dark a certain space is? You measure the amount of light present. Isn't this correct? *Darkness* is a term used by human beings to describe what happens when there is no light present."

The professor just gaped at the young man, who then asked him, "Sir, does evil exist?"

Now uncertain, the professor responded, "Of course, as I have already said. We see it every day. It is in the daily example of the inhumanity humankind is capable of. It is in the multitude of crime and violence everywhere in the world. These manifestations are nothing else but evil."

To this the student replied, "Evil does not exist, sir, or at least it does not exist unto itself. Evil is simply the relative absence of God. It is, just like darkness and cold, a word that human beings created to describe the absence of God. God did not create evil. What we call evil is the result of what happens when a person is unaware of the presence of God's Love in his or her heart. It's like the cold that comes when there is no heat or the darkness that comes when there is no light."

The professor sat down.

This story is attributed to the early university days of Albert Einstein. While we don't know if it's true, it does encompass the premises of Spiritual Psychology.

❧

It's within the context of Love that we have affirmed: *The nature of God is Love! And since we are a part of God, our nature is also Love—regardless of what we believe or how we may behave. Yes, we know that our behavior misrepresents us at times. This doesn't alter the nature of who we are.*

For all practical purposes, spiritual advancement for most people means nothing more than an inner shift to the place inside where they're more aware of the quality of Love that's always present as an internal reality independent of circumstances. For this reason, the vertical extension of the Learning Line has one, and only one, dimension: *Unconditional Love.*

Figure 17

HIGHER SPIRITUAL CONTEXT = LOVE
(Home of the Authentic Self)

It's accurate to say that those who express greater levels of Unconditional Love are further along on the evolutionary ladder. They're people who see past the limitations of the ego-driven, dualistic *perspective*. Metaphorically, they no longer have to be monitored crossing the street because they clearly see the obvious danger of rapidly moving cars.

In a very real sense, the more evolved among us represent our future. The great teachers of the ages have demonstrated the apex of the human evolutionary journey. Henry Miller had this realization when he wrote: "The Buddhas and the Christs are born complete. They neither seek love nor give love, because they are love itself. But we who are born again and again must discover the meaning of love, must learn to live love as the flower lives beauty."

The really good news is that these evolved individuals don't represent a fortunate few. They represent the future and destiny of everyone. In this regard, "heaven" is not a place but a state of consciousness, one where all dualities and perspectives have been surrendered unto God. It's the place where we "live love as the flower lives beauty."

The higher up the evolutionary scale one goes, the more material goals tend to dissolve into spiritual aspirations and a growing awareness of the Divine. All the world's major religions were founded by people who had these realizations as a result of climbing to the higher rungs of the ladder. They didn't simply know this information and choose to behave in the ways they did; rather, they *ascended* in their consciousness to a place where the qualities of the sacred consciousness were woven into the very fabric of their being.

They aligned with the qualities existing in spiritual reality, which emanated from them and could be discerned by others. Such people, like Sadhu Grewal, had *become* the qualities we've ascribed to the Authentic Self level. As we've said, the fundamental one is Love, from which others—such as Peace, Compassion, Joy, Acceptance, and Gratitude—are derived. From their lofty vantage point, these awakened individuals designed pathways to assist those who come after them. These pathways lead ever upward into the higher ground of spiritual reality, toward the ultimate context that embraces all others—usually referred to as *God*.

At the start of a conscious journey into higher levels of Love, an individual consciously chooses to engage in Loving behaviors. One of the most powerful is *Compassionate Self-Forgiveness*. Eventually, such a person becomes Unconditionally Loving, and choice is replaced with a way of Being. Loving people don't choose to be that way any more than they choose to be human. They simply *are!*

The Heart of the Matter

There's one thing we still need to explain further, because a lack of clarification on this point has been a source of human suffering for centuries. As we've mentioned, it's estimated that the birth of the universe occurred some 14 billion years ago. Regardless of the nature of its origin, observation indicates that it's evolving, just as we are. Our premise is that the universe and everything in it is composed of Unconditional Love.

From this basis, it's an easy temptation to jump to the conclusion that it's the degree of Love present that determines one's level of spiritual development. This would be an inaccurate conclusion. If the Absolute embraces all levels or contexts, then Love must be everywhere and present at all times, because that's the nature of the Absolute Context we call *God*. In other words, *Love must sit behind all perspectives and contexts or they couldn't exist, since nothing exists outside of Creation.*

Therefore, it's not the *presence of Love* that defines spiritual growth but the *awareness of the presence of Love*. Less spiritually evolved people aren't inherently less Loving than their more evolved sisters and brothers. Rather, they're simply less aware of the Loving that's their very nature. It's this recognition—that it's the level of awareness that's at issue—that allows the necessary insight and inspiration for moving forward. Can you imagine the radical shift in your life once you become aware that your primary task is to awaken to the vast Loving Essence of who you already are, while also knowing that everyone else is involved in the same journey?

This assumption is basic to Spiritual Psychology. *Our biggest challenge as humans is that we're largely unaware of ourselves as Souls and think that who we are is encompassed in our minds, emotions, and bodies,* which is why the dictionary defines *psychology* as "the science of mind and behavior." In the nondualistic reality of Spiritual Psychology, the entire *Diagnostic and Statistical Manual of Mental Disorders*—which is the manual used by mental-health professionals—could be reduced to a single code. We'd call it "100.1—Perceived Separation from Self." That's Self with a capital *S* to convey the Authentic Self, the one awake in Spirit who speaks when we say, "I Am." It's not the small self, existing in the province of the personality ego that's governed by the mind.

This realization was exquisitely recognized and utilized by Roberto Assagioli in his widely acclaimed psychosynthesis disidentification exercise, which we have adapted at USM as follows:

> I have a body, but I am not my body.
>
> I have feelings, but I am not my feelings.
>
> I have desires, but I am not my desires.
>
> I have a mind, but I am not my mind.
>
> Who am I?
>
> I am myself, a Center of pure Loving Awareness,
> alive in the Peace and Beauty of God's Eternal Love.

If there's one thing we know for sure, it's that as people grow in the awareness of who they are as Loving Beings, they tend to behave in mutually supportive—rather than in warlike—ways just as surely as the growing (evolving) child no longer needs to be told not to run into the path of oncoming traffic. What an extraordinary day it will be when it becomes just as obvious that war is no longer a viable option.

The good news is that people appear to be waking up into a greater awareness of who they are as Loving Beings, and this appears to be happening on a global scale at an accelerated rate. It's clear that something new is struggling to be born in the midst of something old struggling to keep from dying. More good news is that if each person is indeed on an evolutionary journey and Love is already present, then the end is assured. As our beloved friend and spiritual teacher John-Roger is fond of reminding us, "Not one Soul will be lost."

After all, if you're in a spiritual river, even if you swim upstream, the current will eventually carry you to its destination.

Everyone's job is to awaken their awareness into what already is. The upward arrow in Figure 17 aptly represents spiritual progression as a succession of shifts from one context into another, each of which functions at higher and higher frequencies of Love as we all deepen in our awareness of our Divinity. *Healing,* then, describes the process of spiritual progression and is another word for evolution. It's the application of Loving anywhere there's pain. Healing also refers to the process of releasing judgment, thereby automatically alleviating unnecessary emotional suffering and clearing up unresolved issues.

This is all that stands between your ego-centered awareness and the awareness of who you are as a Divine Being having a human experience. The good news is that it's an adventure you will complete. Not only are you designed that way, but it's your *destiny.* All that's really at issue is how long it will take you.

The Unconscious Boulders

Since you've come this far with us, there's one additional piece of information we'd love for you to take with you and reflect upon regularly: If Love encompasses all contexts and is all that is Real, it's impossible to operate outside of Love, regardless of what anyone has thought or done. From our many classes, we've come to realize that along with the normal conscious rocks of everyday judgment that are relatively easy to identify and release, there are some jumbo-sized boulders that reside in the unconscious. These are more difficult to bring to the surface. Their presence is made known when we ask people questions like: "Do you sometimes experience a gnawing sense that somewhere, somehow you did something wrong and you don't know what it is? Have you ever been aware of a lingering sense of shame, guilt, humiliation, self-doubt, and/or unworthiness but you don't know its cause or where it came from?"

It's as if there's a deeply carved flaw somewhere in your very makeup that results in an awful feeling of separation. You may experience a fear that you must have made a huge mistake, but you don't know what. When you search for evidence, perhaps you reason along the lines that here you are in this pitiful human condition, seemingly separated from God, and you must have done something terribly wrong, for which you're being punished . . . but you don't know what you did.

Those who have a dynamic of this nature operating in their unconscious often feel a need to be punished, and if an outside source isn't available, they'll punish themselves with harsh self-criticism or worse. To that end, in USM's prison-service work, it's been sobering for us to discover inmates who feel they rightly deserve to be behind bars based upon their unconscious sense of guilt. (Since 2004, USM has been sending a team of some 50 graduates of the Spiritual Psychology Master's degree Program twice each year to Valley State Prison for Women, one of the largest maximum-security prisons for women in California. The team works for three days with approximately 250 inmates in a workshop entitled Freedom to Choose. A 22-minute on-site documentary can be viewed by going to: **usmfreedomtochoose.net**.)

Herein lies perhaps the biggest misunderstanding humanity labors under—the distinction between having done something for which we deserve to be punished versus having done something that we have the opportunity to learn from and balance. When we see through Soul-Centered Eyes, we realize that reality isn't set up for punishment, but rather with infinite learning opportunities and chances to correct behaviors that result in unwanted consequences. Metaphysically, this action is known as karma. And, as Figure 18 shows, the flip side of the unconscious contains a tremendous repository of unutilized creativity.

While the subject of the unconscious could easily fill a book of its own, our intention here is to provide a useful tool in working with unconscious negative material. The first thing to bear in mind is Principle #2: *The Nature of God is Love!* If this is the case, then what we're talking about is that you've simply lost awareness of your Original Innocence, which by its very nature remains untouched within. In God's eyes, you're loved unconditionally, regardless of your choices and behaviors. You're loved beyond your comprehension and human-made rules. And you're loved enough that you're given infinite opportunities to awaken, to open your spiritual eyes and live in the revelation of your Authentic Self. The Love we're talking about sits behind all experience and just is what it is—God's Nature.

We've done our best to illustrate this in the following figure by showing that God's Love, as represented by the huge heart, encompasses all contexts and levels of consciousness and is truly the essence from which everything is derived.

Figure 18

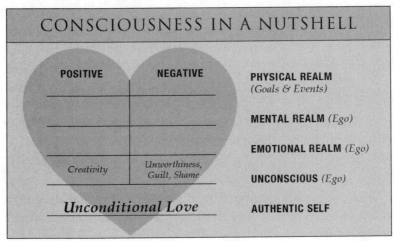

CONSCIOUSNESS IN A NUTSHELL

POSITIVE	NEGATIVE	
		PHYSICAL REALM (*Goals & Events*)
		MENTAL REALM (*Ego*)
		EMOTIONAL REALM (*Ego*)
Creativity	*Unworthiness, Guilt, Shame*	**UNCONSCIOUS** (*Ego*)
Unconditional Love		**AUTHENTIC SELF**

If you can relate to the preceding figure, as many we've asked can, then this is a marvelous opportunity to clearly realize that you are not your thoughts, feelings, or behavior. Rather, you're the Divine Being who is evolving through the experience of your thoughts, feelings, and behavior. As Mary said in an interview pertaining to the Freedom to Choose service project:

> People who are in prison are in a situation where they've received feedback from their universe saying that some of the choices they've made are inappropriate. For most of us who grew up in this culture, we don't clearly distinguish between who we are as a person and behavior or choices that we have made. It's important to clarify that distinction. Who you are as a person is different from the choices you've made, and is different from the behavior in which you've engaged. You can learn to love and accept yourself, you can learn to love and accept your choices, and you can also learn to make different choices.

As you awaken into the context of spiritual reality, you will see that whatever you have thought, felt, or done is all in service to the Learning Line of existence. You made choices that were followed by consequences. While your choices may have contributed to pain for yourself and others, there was never any *wrong* in any of them. Judgment is what locks you in to the self-created prison of *right doing* and *wrong doing* based on ego-centered seeing.

It's for this reason that you willingly enter into *Compassionate Self-Forgiveness* to release yourself from the burdens you've erroneously assigned to yourself. Within this spiritual context, we lovingly invite you to consider the following:

You never did anything "wrong" but that you judged it as wrong.

How could you if your nature is really Love? If what we're saying has any validity for you deep in the recesses of your unconscious, we suggest reciting the following Self-Forgiveness statement: "I forgive myself for ever buying into the illusion that somehow I exist separate from God," or "I forgive myself for any and every judgment I have ever issued, conscious or unconscious, and I step fully into the awareness of who I am—a Divine, Loving Being."

At this point you might be wondering, *If I'm a Divine, Loving Being and always have been, since that's my inherent nature, how could I ever have placed all these rocks in my backpack in the first place?* That is a magnificent question, which is wonderfully answered by the poet Dorothea Bisbas in her poem entitled "What He Carried."

> *He shifts the backpack between*
> *his chafing blades, rubbed raw*
> *from its oppressive weight,*
> *his head a rigid thunderbolt*
> *surging charges of terror through*
> *his mind, un-nameable fears.*
> *Cleats bruise the snow.*
> *Ropes and pick-ax ready for the final climb.*
> *He shrugs to rearrange his load,*
> *now a familiar hump,*
> *one he has carried for years,*
> *one he thinks he was born with.*
> *In this altitude his breath labors,*
> *freezing before him in exhaled clouds,*
> *eyes no longer able to see beyond*
> *his own footstep,*
> *the icy Everest slick and slippery*
> *its pinnacle always out of reach.*
>
> *When they find him frozen in the crags,*
> *they remove his backpack,*
> *astonished to discover,*
> *the unbearable weight of emptiness.*

(From the collection of Rancho Mirage 2010–2012 Poet Laureate Dorothea Bisbas, poetry workshop facilitator for Rancho Mirage Library; poem used with permission.)

What Dorothea is saying, and what's foundational to Spiritual Psychology, is that judgments are ego created and exist in the illusory world of duality. When you see through Soul-Centered Eyes, you realize that judgments have no existence in the reality of the Authentic Self. They do not and cannot exist in the energy field of Love. This is an essential realization resulting in a shift in awareness from ego-centered reality to Soul-Centered reality. *And yes, this means that all judgments are made of nothing. That is why they dissolve in Love.*

Thus, we have come to the 22nd principle of Spiritual Psychology:

> **Principle #22:** *Judgment is self-condemnation.*
> *Self-Forgiveness is redemption; and Compassion,*
> *Acceptance, Peace, and Joy naturally follow.*

I look forward to the day when I ask my Soul, "Who are you?" and it replies not with "I am a ghost bound to a very small world," but with "I am who I am, free and Home." As John-Roger puts it:

> *When we get high enough in the*
> *Consciousness of God,*
> *we all have the same name.*
> *And that name is "Love."*

Might John-Roger be echoing the description of the Authentic Self as expressed by the 13th-century Persian poet Rumi, who said: "Out beyond ideas of right doing and wrong doing there lies a field . . . I'll meet you there"? After all, it's a valid question for the ego to ask, "Once we forgive, then what? Who will we be if we let go of our judgments? What happens when we all meet in Rumi's field?"

Our answer is: *Let's go there and find out for our Selves!* One thing's for sure—there will certainly be an abundance of Unconditional Love present. And to get there, we'll probably be engaging in a fair amount of *Compassionate Self-Forgiveness* along the way.

Once you've completed your work of letting go, you'll walk through life in Acceptance. Since you'll make no judgments, there will be no unnecessary emotional suffering, and no Self-Forgiveness will be required. Your backpack will be empty, and having learned the art of Acceptance, you'll live in Peace and no longer be involved in rock collecting.

At that amazing time, the path of your life will be revealed in stunning clarity—its direction readily apparent, requiring little navigation. You'll meet other conscious travelers along the way, and as you pass, you'll each bow your head in Namaste . . . and your greeting to each other, rather than "How are you?" will be "Thank you for being Loyal to your Soul."

Stem Sentences to Write Down and Contemplate

• For me, Loyalty to my Soul means . . .

Repeat as often as necessary.

AFTERWORD

As we come to the completion of writing *Loyalty to Your Soul,* our hearts are filled with the Spirit of Gratitude. For the two of us, the principles and practices of Spiritual Psychology have not only informed our lives, but also radically transformed them. What began more than 30 years ago as an interesting field of study has, like any worthwhile practice, become a way of life.

We're writing this Afterword sitting in the back of the classroom during the seventh month of a USM first-year class in the Spiritual Psychology Master's degree Program. We're observing 12 groups, each consisting of 20 people. On cue, one by one, each student is presenting to his or her classmates. Their presentations consist of their individual approaches to the art of shifting into greater awareness of themselves as Divine Beings having a human experience. The creativity of each student's approach is amazing to behold. We're in awe as we witness the individualized emergence of each person who enthusiastically embraces a newfound spiritual adventure. Ah, the wonders of Soul-Centered experiential education.

But now what?

As we all know, reading and agreeing with principles, concepts, and ideas is one thing; living into them—embracing them as a way of being, a way of life—is quite another. As we say in Principle #6: *Spiritual evolution (growth) is a process, not an event.* Or perhaps more fitting, *Loyalty to Your Soul* is a process, not an event.

There are some obvious ways you can more fully integrate the material presented in this book, beginning with the stem sentences you wrote. If you haven't done that part of the process, we suggest you review each chapter and complete these over the course of the next few days or weeks. The completed statements can simply be the beginning of a journal, and you can continually add to it every day or week. Your responses over time may reflect a measure of your spiritual growth and increasing commitment to awakening into your Authentic Self.

Then, of course, there are the 22 principles of *Seeing Through Soul-Centered Eyes*. By simply reflecting upon a particular challenge in your life, you may find that one or more of the principles provides you with inspiration or direction regarding that situation. *Seeing Through Soul-Centered Eyes* makes all the difference, as that perspective will often guide you into a Learning Orientation to Life—so essential when traveling upward on the Learning Line of spiritual evolution.

And by all means, we encourage you to utilize the *Soul-Centered Practices*. They have a 30-year proven track record of producing results. We, along with thousands of USM grads, utilize these principles and practices each day.

Thank you for allowing us to share some of the blessings of Spiritual Psychology with you. The empowering perspectives and tools offered within these pages can profoundly change your life and open you to a greater awareness of who you are, why you're here, and how you can live a more meaningful and fulfilling life. After all, you're a Divine Being having a human experience. Why not live more like one as you learn to utilize your everyday experiences as rungs of the ladder of your spiritual awakening? May these principles and practices assist you in that process!

As you go forward in your spiritual evolution, as you surely will, we encourage you to remember that growing spiritually isn't a function of greater understanding—although greater understanding occurs as you grow. Rather, *spiritual evolution* is more akin to a place within that allows you to suddenly open yourself to receiving Grace—an awareness of Love that you've never previously experienced. At the same time, spiritual evolution slowly seeps into every crack and crevice of your life, and you slowly shift from saying the true answer to *living* the true answer.

May your life be blessed with ever-increasing awareness of who you truly are.

— **Ron** and **Mary Hulnick**
Santa Monica, California

Appendix A

The Principles of Spiritual Psychology

Chapter 1

1. *We are not human beings with Souls; we are Souls having a human experience.*

Chapter 2

2. *The nature of God is Love!*

3. *Direct experience is the process through which belief or faith is transformed into knowing.*

4. *Since we are all part of God, our nature also is Love, and we have the opportunity to know our Loving nature experientially, here and now!*

Chapter 3

5. *Physical-world reality exists for the purpose of spiritual evolution.*

6. *Spiritual evolution (growth) is a process, not an event.*

7. *All of life is for Learning.*

Chapter 4

8. *An unresolved issue is anything that disturbs your peace.*

9. *Every time a single person resolves a single issue, angels rejoice and all of humanity moves forward in its evolution.*

Chapter 5

10. *All "becauses" are merely triggers to internal unresolved issues inviting completion.*

11. *Inner disturbances are themselves a major component of the spiritual curriculum you are here to complete.*

12. *Unresolved issues are not bad; they are just part of your spiritual curriculum and are an opportunity for healing.*

13. *Personal responsibility is the foundational key that opens the door to Freedom.*

14. *Nothing outside of you causes your disturbances.*

Chapter 6

15. *You create your future by how you respond to experiences now.*

16. *How you relate to an issue is the issue, and how you relate to yourself while you go through an issue is the issue.*

Chapter 7

17. *What you believe determines your experience.*

Chapter 8

18. *A life filled with Acceptance is a life devoid of unnecessary emotional suffering. It's a life filled with Love.*

19. *Your primary goal is not to change the school; your primary goal is to graduate.*

Chapter 9

20. *Healing is the application of Loving to the places inside that hurt.*

21. *Loving, Healing, and Evolving are all the same process.*

Chapter 10

22. *Judgment is self-condemnation. Self-Forgiveness is redemption; and Compassion, Acceptance, Peace, and Joy naturally follow.*

Appendix B

Summary of Soul-Centered Practices

We thought you might like to have the five Soul-Centered Practices in one place for easy reference without the examples. In this way, they're ready for your use whenever you need them.

Seeing the Loving Essence and Heart-Centered Listening

1. Center your awareness in your heart and consciously look for the Loving Essence in the person in your presence. By doing so, you're signifying your respect for the Soul before you, regardless of who the person is, his or her situation or circumstances, or the nature of your relationship.

2. Maintain awareness that you're in conversation with another Divine Being who is engaged in having a human experience. Remember that as a Soul, the other person has all the inner resources necessary to effectively respond to his or her situation.

3. Set your intention to open yourself to look with the eyes of your heart and listen with the ears of your heart.

4. Give the person before you your full attention, your respect, and your caring. (No meaningful conversation is ever going to occur while the TV is on.)

5. Follow his or her lead. Listen at all four levels: *content, tonality,* to the *person,* and for his or her *meaning.*

6. Assist the other person in giving dimension and depth to what is shared through the use of minimal encouragement such as, "I really hear you. Would you like to say a bit more about that?"

7. Support the individual in completing one topic before going on to the next. The more information people share at one time, the more difficult it can be to follow them and effectively respond to all that they're saying.

8. Resist the urge to give advice. You are engaging in *Seeing the Loving Essence* and *Heart-Centered Listening!*

Facilitating Responsibility I: Choice

1. Center your awareness in your heart and consciously look for the Loving Essence within. Allow yourself to identify a current situation that you would like to be different.

2. Are you aware of any choices (inner and/or outer) you're presently making that tend to maintain the situation as it is?

3. Take your time and consider the possibility of other choices that might produce different results. It's not that you have to do anything differently; can you simply see any alternatives?

4. Without committing to doing anything different at this time, take a few minutes and visualize yourself in the process of making the new choices in the present, as if you were making them now.

Facilitating Responsibility II: Ownership

1. Center your awareness in your heart and consciously look for the Loving Essence within. Allow yourself to identify a recent experience where you found yourself experiencing emotional distress and wanting to blame yourself or someone else for what happened and for your reaction.

2. Utilizing the Soul-Centered Practices of *Seeing the Loving Essence* and *Heart-Centered Listening,* and without trying to change anything, allow yourself to move into a place of Acceptance: Acceptance of what is; of your feelings; of your actions; and even of any conclusions you may have drawn about yourself, others, and/or your experience.

3. Once you've entered a place of Acceptance, allow yourself to accept ownership of your feelings and actions without blaming anyone, especially yourself. Remember that no matter what you did, how you felt at the time, or how you're feeling right now, you're still a beautiful, valuable, and lovable Soul who's truly doing your best.

4. Gently remind yourself that anytime you feel upset, all that has happened is that your spiritual agenda is revealing places in your consciousness that are in need of healing, and that these situations are God-given opportunities for progressing spiritually.

Transforming Limiting Beliefs

1. Center your awareness in your heart and consciously look for the Loving Essence within. Bring to mind a situation that triggered a negative emotional reaction inside of you. It's best to select a recent one that's still fresh in your consciousness. What happened? How did you feel? What did you do in response?

2. Assuming the premise that underlying every feeling is a belief and/or value, what were your definitions of reality associated with this situation?

3. Is there another perspective you *could* choose to hold about this situation that you anticipate would result in a more positive feeling? If so, what might it be?

4. If you held this new perspective, how do you suppose the situation might have turned out differently?

Compassionate Self-Forgiveness

1. Center your awareness in your heart and consciously look for the Loving Essence within. Bring to mind a recent situation that triggered a negative emotional reaction inside of you. What happened? How did you feel? What did you do in response?

2. Give your feelings a voice. Let the hurt or angry part inside speak freely, and write down what it says. Don't censor your expression, and don't be concerned with grammar or spelling. Allow the "I am upset because . . ." voice to speak freely.

3. Move into a place of accepting yourself, your feelings, and the situation as a God-given opportunity that's present for your learning and growth.

4. Take 100 percent responsibility for your emotional reaction as a way of reclaiming dominion inside yourself and over the situation.

5. List any judgments against others and yourself that you perceive are present. They're usually easily identified from Step 2. They're condemning, or "wrong-making," statements.

6. Engage in Compassionate Self-Forgiveness for your judgments.

7. When you're finished, move into your Authentic Self, a place of Self-Acceptance and Self-Compassion, as best you know how. Ask yourself what the Truth is about this situation.

8. Once the negative energy has lifted and you're back in balance, look for creative solutions to the triggering situation for the highest good of all concerned. They'll usually be right there. Effective outer action follows successful inner action.

9. Acknowledge and appreciate yourself for your willingness to learn how to work with your disturbance as an opportunity for growth and healing.

Acknowledgments

We're deeply grateful to the people who have supported us in writing *Loyalty to Your Soul:*

To all those who have been students in our classes over the past 30 years, whose deep sharing and joy of learning have touched our hearts and inspired our thinking.

To our beloved friend and colleague Johanna Jenkins for reading the original manuscript and offering her wise counsel and feedback.

To our personal editor, Nancy O'Leary, whose enthusiasm for this subject matter and keen attention to detail guided us through the narrows to completion.

To Licia Rester-Frazee, our dear friend and faculty member, for reviewing an early draft and providing feedback in service to our clarifying the concepts to make them readily accessible for the readers.

To Sherry Johannes, whose design gifts have graced the book cover as well as these pages with divine inspiration.

To our esteemed colleague Neale Donald Walsch, for his heartfelt support and encouragement.

To our good friend Steve Chandler, who encouraged us to put into words the essentials of Spiritual Psychology.

To everyone on the faculty and staff of the University of Santa Monica who believed in us, supported us, and generously put their love and gifts into this work.

To the members of the Hay House staff—Reid Tracy, Patrick Gabrysiak, Alex Freemon, and Jill Kramer—for their belief in us and this project and their significant contributions to it emerging in completed form.

To Spirit for blessing us, guiding us, inspiring us, and supporting us throughout. We are so grateful.

And to John-Roger, whose loving support has made all the difference. Thank you for teaching us to be loyal to our Souls.

About the Authors

Drs. Ron and **Mary Hulnick** are world-renowned educators and pioneers in the emerging field of Spiritual Psychology. As founding faculty and co-directors of the University of Santa Monica (USM), they have designed, and continue to facilitate, the life-changing experiential Master's degree Program in Spiritual Psychology, which they define as the study and practice of the art and science of human evolution in consciousness.

USM, recognized as the Worldwide Center for the Study & Practice of Spiritual Psychology™, offers its programs within the context of Soul-Centered education. This philosophy acknowledges spiritual reality and begins with the assumption that we are not human beings who have a soul; we are souls having a human experience. The goal of the educational process is to bring forth the beauty, wisdom, and compassion inherent in every human being.

Both Ron and Mary are licensed Marriage and Family Therapists in California, and Mary is also a licensed Clinical Psychologist. They are the executive producers of, and appear in, the award-winning documentary *Freedom to Choose,* which is based on USM's seven-year service project at Valley State Prison for Women in Chowchilla, California.

They have been happily married for 32 years and reside with their beloved cat, Sweetstuff, in Los Angeles, California.

Websites: **www.universityofsantamonica.edu** and **www.LoyaltyToYourSoul.com**

NOTES

NOTES

NOTES

NOTES

NOTES

NOTES

NOTES

NOTES

Notes

NOTES

NOTES

NOTES

We hope you enjoyed this Hay House book. If you'd like to receive our online catalog featuring additional information on Hay House books and products, or if you'd like to find out more about the Hay Foundation, please contact:

Hay House, Inc.
P.O. Box 5100
Carlsbad, CA 92018-5100

(760) 431-7695 or **(800) 654-5126**
(760) 431-6948 (fax) or **(800) 650-5115 (fax)**
www.hayhouse.com® • **www.hayfoundation.org**

ↁↁ

Published and distributed in Australia by: Hay House Australia Pty. Ltd., 18/36 Ralph St., Alexandria NSW 2015 • *Phone:* 612-9669-4299 *Fax:* 612-9669-4144 • www.hayhouse.com.au

Published and distributed in the United Kingdom by: Hay House UK, Ltd., 292B Kensal Rd., London W10 5BE • *Phone:* 44-20-8962-1230 *Fax:* 44-20-8962-1239 • www.hayhouse.co.uk

Published and distributed in the Republic of South Africa by: Hay House SA (Pty), Ltd., P.O. Box 990, Witkoppen 2068 • *Phone/Fax:* 27-11-467-8904 info@hayhouse.co.za • www.hayhouse.co.za

Published in India by: Hay House Publishers India, Muskaan Complex, Plot No. 3, B-2, Vasant Kunj, New Delhi 110 070 • *Phone:* 91-11-4176-1620 *Fax:* 91-11-4176-1630 • www.hayhouse.co.in

Distributed in Canada by: Raincoast, 9050 Shaughnessy St., Vancouver, B.C. V6P 6E5 • *Phone:* (604) 323-7100 • *Fax:* (604) 323-2600 • www.raincoast.com

ↁↁ

Take Your Soul on a Vacation

Visit **www.HealYourLife.com®** to regroup, recharge, and reconnect with your own magnificence. Featuring blogs, mind-body-spirit news, and life-changing wisdom from Louise Hay and friends.

Visit **www.HealYourLife.com** today!